WASHINGTON'S

SCONES

T0274701

WASHINGTON'S

Fisher® SCONES

· AN ICONIC NORTHWEST TREAT SINCE 1911 ·

JIM ERICKSON

AMERICAN PALATE

Published by American Palate, a Division of The History Press
Charleston, SC
www.historypress.com

Front, top right: A hot table worker offers a tasty scone for a loyal customer. *Photo by author; front, bottom left*: Two scones buttered and jammed are ready to bring satisfaction. *Photo by Keith Erickson; back, bottom center*: The Fisher logo is recognized at fairs, special events and on a food truck because of its favorite treat. *Courtesy Conifer Specialties*.

First published 2023

Manufactured in the United States

ISBN 9781467153010

Library of Congress Control Number: 2022951604

Notice: The information in this book is true and complete to the best of our knowledge. It is offered without guarantee on the part of the author or The History Press. The author and The History Press disclaim all liability in connection with the use of this book.

Dedicated to my wife, Pam, and sons, Keith and Gregg,
for their constant support and input to make this book the best it could be.

CONTENTS

PREFACE

You wouldn't believe what people do for two and a half ounces of dough, a dollop of butter and a glop of raspberry jam. Some wait in line for an hour and then only order one item made from those ingredients. Why? Because the item is the famous Fisher Fair Scone, a legendary biscuit served throughout the Pacific Northwest since 1911 and one for which the collective appetite of folks has never waned. It is as popular today as it was in the last century, maybe even more so, despite some caveats. Yes, you have people complaining, "These scones are smaller than I remember." Others chiming in, "And I could buy one for a quarter." As a veteran scone maker of nearly two decades, I have to smile and reassure these individuals that a scone is still a tasty treat at a more reasonable price than other dessert fare and politely and humorously correct memories about the scones' size: "Well, sir, I can surely tell you with confidence that a scone was never, ever as big as a hubcap." The two and a half ounces of dough for each scone is determined by the process. When the dough is made in a large mixer and a huge pile dumped on a table, the dough maker weighs a ball of ten ounces (with never more than ten and a half as a margin of error for convenience sake), rolls each ball smooth, flattens it and uses a cutter to make four equally sized dough triangles. The cut has to be precise, however, because if it isn't, then two of the dough pieces will be smaller than the other two. But if you've done dough long enough, for many years, you can make that exact cut without any problem. Then there's the jam. It's always been raspberry jam, never anything else. Not strawberry. Not blackberry.

Not peanut butter. But some customers ask what kind of scones we have. We reply, "Butter and raspberry jam." And, perhaps, on occasion add that it's been only raspberry since 1911. I recall one time, someone asked for orange marmalade, to which another scone worker gasped, "What's that?" While some folks order only one scone, there are others who desire more, ordering multiples, or even as many as a baker's dozen. "How many are in a baker's dozen?" people frequently ask. "Thirteen for certain," we quip, "but maybe more if the baker's counting. That's why we call it a baker's dozen." Because I began my early scone days as the baker, sometimes I share the origin of the baker's dozen, explaining that it dates back to medieval times when bakers erred on the side of giving an extra food item to a regular dozen to ensure the customer received the specific weight total guaranteed by law. Violation of the law resulted in dire punishment for the baker. The practice goes back even further. In Egypt, a baker shorting customers lost an ear that consequently got nailed to the exterior of his shop. In Babylon, a cheating baker lost a hand. We always take a baker's dozen seriously, even though we're not about to get punished. We just like to give customers a deal for buying that number of scones.

These are all facts that most scone workers know and information that many customers know if they've eaten scones when they were kids and introduced scones to their kids and so forth. Generations of people enjoying scones. So, why do a book on Fisher scones? Ask, instead, Why not? The story of Fisher scones is a good one and it's never been done. With my journalism background and my experience making and selling Fisher scones, it seemed that I had the right combination to write this book. But I couldn't have done it without the help of my son Keith, who has worked scones as long as I have and has incredible research skills and a keen awareness of the importance of history. Using my digging skills, I was able to delve into the past to pull out information on the early life of the Fisher family back in the mid- to late nineteenth century. A Fisher family history and genealogy book was helpful in detailing the early life of O.W. Fisher, his sawmill and flour mill experiences and his wife, sons, daughter and subsequent generations. Searching old newspapers through newspapers.com was useful in finding out how the Fisher family promoted Fisher's Blend flour and Fisher scones, particularly in the first three decades of the twentieth century. The Northwest Room of the Tacoma Public Library found and created photos of advertisements in Tacoma newspapers in the 1930s featuring a resourceful, young home economist who took the stage name Mary Mills to revise Fisher recipe books using Fisher's Blend flour, and she promoted the mills' products. Fortunately,

I had the opportunity to interview a woman whose mother was the first Mary Mills, and I am also grateful for an interview with Phelps Fisher, who shared his stories of the Fisher Mills and Fisher's broadcast empire.

But it was Keith who was amazing. He continually found little nuggets that I believe nobody else could have gotten, vital stories and photos that seemed to be buried forever (e.g., Fisher Flour Mills sponsored an amateur hockey team in the 1930s). Furthermore, Keith won auction items or bought stuff outright that gave me a memorabilia collection from which to obtain information and images for use in a scone book. Those included a decades-old cloth flour bag, Fisher recipe books from the 1930s, glassine bags in which individual scones were inserted, a historic ad from a 1919 magazine touting Paul's Jam used in the first scones ever made and postcards depicting such pictures as the Fisher Mills on Harbor Island in Seattle in 1911, TV star Betty White's recipe cards for orange and banana loaves using Fisher's Blend flour and Fisher's own rail line at a Louisiana sawmill operation. Surprisingly, historical museums in western Washington counties and numerous fairs had little historical data regarding Fisher scones in their particular venues. At one point, I uttered a frustrated comment to a curator of a prestigious history museum, "I feel like an explorer." She laughed and replied, "I know what you mean." It was so rewarding when Keith and I found some facts, photos, or stories that were unique because it encouraged us to continue to seek the truth out there. We became so enlightened, so fascinated with what we were finding that we had to go on, probably much like prospectors who found gold in a stream or a mine and were spurred to keep searching. We were also motivated because we knew that the many scone-loving readers with sweet memories would enjoy a book about the history and stories behind their favorite tasty treat. Just like us.

Jim Erickson
November 2022

ACKNOWLEDGEMENTS

Thanks go out to Pat Heily of the Heily family, owners of Conifer Specialties and Continental Mills (now the Krusteaz Company), for his support and "green light" to proceed on a book about the history of Fisher scones, something never done before.

Finding a research tool that could be used to gather the information and stories was crucial to the effort, and I was fortunate to find one in newspapers. com, a valuable resource that allowed me to delve into newspapers dating back more than one hundred years.

My sons, Keith and Gregg, proved invaluable. Keith continually searched to find all kinds of stories that couldn't be found anywhere else and was able to acquire items through auctions or outright purchases that built an Erickson collection usable in the scone book. Many of his own photos help illustrate the book. Gregg was my advisor and technical troubleshooter.

A special shout-out goes to Ilona Perry and the research team at the Northwest Room of the Tacoma Public Library for truly amazing help that got me some historical images that were painstakingly rescanned to make them work in the book. I am so appreciative.

In addition, it was essential to get the stories of people—workers and customers—who remembered Fisher scones.

My son Keith and I first interviewed and photographed Suzanne Hall, daughter of the first Mary Mills, who promoted Fisher Flour in the 1930s, and after Hall died a month later, I took scones to her celebration of life and learned more about the generosity she extended to everyone all her life.

I was fortunate to find and interview Phelps Fisher, great-grandson of Oliver Williams (O.W.) Fisher, patriarch of the Fisher family. I appreciated Phelps's insight recalling some of the early days of the Fisher Flouring Mills and Fisher's growing empire, including the broadcast industry. A treasure-trove of knowledge that impressed me. Through Phelps, I learned about the strong support that his wife, Christel, provided for him and the entire Fisher family.

Ken Zugner, a dedicated Conifer employee, holds a special place with me because he hired my son and me to make and sell scones. Under Ken's tutelage, we learned how to do the job of making dough and buttering and jamming the proper way. He earns my respect for all he's done to make Conifer successful over many years.

A.J. Milliken is the consummate scone manager. My son and I worked for him, primarily at the South Building at the Washington State Fair, and know firsthand his skills. Thanks, A.J., for sharing a slice of your food industry experience and savvy perspectives that have helped efficiently run a crew and your permission to use materials from your scone collection in this book. It means a lot.

Of course, getting to Mike Maher, president and CEO of Conifer Specialties, was vital to telling the story of Conifer taking over Fisher's product line, especially Fisher scones, and keeping this precious pastry available for scone lovers throughout the region. Thanks, Mike, for the interview and your expression of unceasing love for Fisher scones.

To others whom I interviewed, I extend my gratitude: Leona Elder for her under-the-grandstand dedication; Kathie Denton for her love of helping people develop scone skills; Kristen Clare for her "mother" qualities as she worked with such joy; Frances and Dwayne Ryland for tales of scones in Oregon; Sally and Howard Lonn for sharing miniature scone booths; Wayne and Robin Osborn for recalling fundraising events selling scones; Emily Campen for remembering her winning guess regarding sale of the 100 millionth scone; John and Kimberly Wrede for telling how they shared scones with friends and workers; and Doug and Lois Quayle for explaining how they gave scones to two hikers on the Pacific Crest Trail at Chinook Pass.

Thank you, Carrie Larson, social media coordinator for Conifer, for organizing and running a contest during the 2022 Washington State Fair to receive favorite scone stories from people via Facebook, with winners getting free scones and being mentioned in my scone book.

Kudos to neighbors Ted and Mary Coyle for using the 1930s *Fisher's Blend Cookbook* to make peanut butter cookies and brownies so I could prove those recipes are still delicious today.

Special recognition goes to a worldwide expert on bulgur wheat—Dr. Mustafa Bayram, dean and professor in the Department of Food Engineering at the University of Gaziantep in Turkey. Dr. Bayram explained the meaning of the term *ala* in reference to bulgur wheat.

My gratitude goes out to Kate Becker, creative economy and recovery director of King County, for conducting a tour that showcased Harbor Island Studios' massive sound stage, an example of a new life on the Fisher Mills site. Thanks to those joining me in the tour group—Mike Blair, Frank Blazkiewicz, A.J. Milliken and my son Keith.

Edit. Edit. Edit. Any writing project needs good editors. Virginia Lane and Mike Blair offered pertinent suggestions in reviewing my manuscript, assisting with readability and the flow of pieces that make up the whole.

Finally, there are so many other scone-loving workers and friends that I cannot name them all, but I appreciate our past connections that have influenced me in writing a book on the history of Fisher scones.

INTRODUCTION

I f you're satisfied just enjoying a warm Fisher scone with butter and raspberry jam and that's it, well good for you. If you've wondered about the story behind the famous pastry item that people throughout the Pacific Northwest have eaten for more than a century, then dig in to this tasty tale. It all began with Oliver Williams Fisher, a man of Scottish ancestry who went by his initials, O.W., throughout his lifetime but who worked hard from the time he was eight years old, when his father, Peter, died. O.W. fought in the Union army during the Civil War and worked at or ran sawmills and flour mills in the central and western parts of the United States for decades before founding the Fisher Flouring Mills on Seattle's Harbor Island in 1911 with his son Oliver David (O.D.) Fisher. The venture was a huge success, and Fisher scones were introduced at the Panama-Pacific Exposition in San Francisco in 1915 and given away as a means of promoting the company's Fisher's Blend flour. It also marked the introduction of an African American baker/chef, Newton Coleman, as the lead person orchestrating the company's marketing effort. *Little House on the Prairie* author Laura Ingalls Wilder enjoyed the scones while visiting her daughter and wrote about them upon returning to Missouri. A founder of the Puyallup Valley Fair discovered them, too, and convinced Fisher officials to bring the scones to its 1915 fair with a promise that he would provide the jam. Mount Rainier provided an awesome backdrop for the Puyallup-Sumner Valley, where the berries were grown to make the jam. Fisher scones are as iconic as the 14,411-foot mountain. Fisher began taking scones to countless fairs up and down the West Coast. Coleman was an instrumental part of that endeavor until his death in 1922. For two years in the mid-1920s, the company even sailed to Hawaii with four ovens to bake scones and promote its flour at two different fairs, setting up a distribution network. In the 1930s, Fisher turned to a series of "Mary Mills" characters to reach out to families and to revise Fisher cookbooks with recipes for cakes, cookies, pastries and other essentials using Fisher flour. The Great Depression and World War II provided challenges, but Fisher prevailed. Fisher continued to travel to fairs, expositions and events in the 1950s, 1960s and 1970s before relinquishing its product line to Continental Mills and Conifer Specialties in 1977. And the scones lived on.

Continue filling your scone appetite with the story of Mike Maher, who started at Conifer as a young man and has become president and CEO of the company. He says some fairs have been dropped over the years, but other events and festivals have been added to keep the schedule at virtually the same number today as in 1977. As long as the fair in Puyallup, known as the Washington State Fair, continues, Fisher scones will stay around, he believes. There are more tales from scone workers, such as Leona Elder, longtime manager under the grandstand at the fairgrounds in Puyallup. Others with memories include Kathie Denton, A.J. Milliken and Kristin Clare. Customers, of course, have memories, and Conifer ran a contest during the 2022 state fair on its Facebook page to solicit stories. Because people have loved Fisher scones for generations and passed that affection on to subsequent family members, the demand has continued. And the scones lived on.

For further fulfillment, read about Phelps Fisher, oldest living family member, who recalls his days as a messenger and broom sweeper at the Fisher Flouring Mills and his switch to the broadcast side and eventual rise to chairman of the board and Emmy winner for helping build a prestigious news crew at KOMO-TV in Seattle. Then, there's Suzanne Hall, daughter of the first "Mary Mills" who promoted Fisher flour. Hall recalled that her mother met gangster Al Capone while doing an internship at a Chicago hospital before her "Mary Mills" job. Hall baked scones for her mother's funeral. Hall died a month after the author interviewed her, and the author brought Fisher scones to her celebration of life ceremony. It seemed like the right thing to do. And the scones lived on.

The author offers his thoughts and memories from nearly two decades working with scones and particularly remembers the workers and customers and some amusing anecdotes that cannot be forgotten. He believes Conifer's food truck was a lifesaver during the COVID-19 pandemic when fairs and other events were shut down in 2020 and 2021. People were grateful that the scone truck was out and about at various places in western Washington, taking it to the streets, so to speak, bringing scones to people in Puyallup, Bonney Lake, Enumclaw, Auburn, Seattle, Bellevue, Tacoma, Lacey, Olympia, Key Peninsula and other places. It kept Conifer vibrant during a really tough time. And it made people appreciate a tasty morsel that they had come to love and enjoy for so many years. It was a source of comfort for people, and they believe it will continue to be comfort food now that the fairs and other events have reopened. And the scones will live on.

PART I

BEGINNING:
EARLY FISHER HISTORY

O.W. Fisher, a Man for His Time

Getting a Foothold in the First Fifty Years of an Ever-Changing Life

When did the connection with scones begin for O.W. Fisher, patriarch of the Fisher family renowned for its longtime ownership and operation of the Fisher Flouring Mills on Seattle's Harbor Island? Did it begin long before the mills opened in 1911, when as a child in the 1840s, he was served a scone by his parents, Peter and Lucretia Fisher? After all, his father, Peter, was, in 1805, born into a family that was running the Royal Hotel in Dunkeld, Scotland. The origin of scones is traced to Scotland in the 1500s and first mentioned by Scottish poet Gavin Douglas in 1513. Scones became a delicacy and national tradition often served morning, noon and evening with butter, jam and clotted cream. It is not unlikely that scones were served to guests at Scottish hotels, including the Royal Hotel, or that Peter Fisher may have eaten one, two or more in the early part of his life. Peter Fisher immigrated to the United States, but there's no record when. Nor is there a record that his parents went with him to America at all. One could assume he was an adult at the time. Records show that Peter Fisher and Lucretia Dodge were married in Portsmouth, Ohio, a town on the Ohio River, on March 8, 1837. Portsmouth was her home; she was born there in 1816. Peter and Lucretia lived there for a while and then moved to Wheelersburg, upriver from Portsmouth. O.W. (Oliver Williams) was born in Wheelersburg in 1842, the fourth of six children, with three brothers older and a brother and sister younger. The "Williams" in his name came from the family of Lucretia's great-grandmother, the wife of American Revolutionary War soldier Jonathan Dodge. Peter worked as a carpenter, and the family struggled in an impoverished area of Ohio; however, even poor people could have gotten flour and made scones, and it's possible that O.W. might have eaten them. The family's struggles intensified after Peter died in 1850. O.W. and his other brothers were forced to go to work for meager wages, certainly no more than two or three dollars a week, likely in jobs at farms along the river or at portable sawmill sites. These were hard times, but O.W. didn't complain. He worked hard. In 1854, he became an apprentice to Uriah Nurse to learn the milling trade, and stayed with him for three years in an occupation he admitted to liking very much. Fisher, now fifteen, moved on, to Springville, a tiny village in Kentucky Bluegrass Country, continuing that line of work at a gristmill grinding grain into flour. Three years later, he returned to his Ohio home to work at a circular sawmill operation.

War was on the horizon, however, and inevitable decisions were imminent. In 1862, Fisher followed his older brothers in joining the Union army and being officially mustered into the Thirty-Ninth Ohio Infantry on September 3, a day after his twentieth birthday. The Civil War had been going on for nearly seventeen months. The Thirty-Ninth Ohio Infantry was made up of woodsmen and farmers lacking the "spit and polish" of soldiers trained in the East. But they made up for their undisciplined manner, exemplified by a casual greeting to an officer rather than a salute. They accomplished that through their natural ability to succeed in the field. They were resourceful, they were accustomed to an outdoor life and they could live off the land as they marched. They knew how to fire a gun long before they donned uniforms. Together, they were a real fighting machine. Few had deep convictions about slavery, but they were strongly in agreement that the Union must not be broken. That was the army in which O.W. Fisher served. The Thirty-Ninth Ohio Infantry was part of General Ulysses S. Grant's army and was stationed at Corinth, located in the northeastern section of the state of Mississippi, under the command of General William Rosecrans. Grant had ordered Rosecrans to hold Corinth at all costs because it was a rail center vital to the Union's campaign against the Confederate army. Fisher first saw action after General Sterling Price moved his rebel army to Iuka, 22 miles southeast of Corinth, and General Earl Van Dorn was in the process of marching his rebel forces to reinforce Price's maneuver. Grant ordered Rosecrans to attack Iuka, and Rosecrans responded quickly, soundly thrashing Price's army on September 19 and forcing them to retreat. Fisher and the Thirty-Ninth Ohio Infantry got into the fray near the end of the battle, when the victory had already been secured. Rosecrans's army returned to Corinth and was attacked by the joint forces of Price and Van Dorn, under command of the latter on October 3. Outnumbered and losing early to the rebels, the Union soldiers began holding their own, waiting for Rosecrans to choose the right time to release what he termed his "thunderbolt." That came on the second day of fighting (October 4) after his men had pushed back the Confederates at a battery called Robinett near the center of the Union line. The thunderbolt was a brigade led by General David Sloane Stanley, which included the Thirty-Ninth Ohio Infantry, in a bayonet charge that swept the Confederates from the battlefield in great confusion, sealing the victory and resulting in a crowning moment in what was, at that point in time, the Civil War's fiercest battle. Fisher faced two battles in his first month of service, but his active duty in the Union army ended after nine months and he returned to Portsmouth, resuming work in a gristmill.

In the spring of 1865, wanderlust struck Fisher. He had a longing to see other parts of America beyond his small scope of existence in Ohio and Kentucky, a notion sharpened by his army experiences in Mississippi

O.W. Fisher and his Union army comrades led a bayonet charge at Corinth, Mississippi, that drove the Confederate army off the battlefield to secure a victory early in the Civil War. *Library of Congress/Currier & Ives.*

and Tennessee. So, he traveled west by rail to St. Joseph, Missouri, the outfitting point and the start of most overland treks across the western United States. A giant of a man for his time—six foot two, weighing 190 pounds, physically strong—Fisher had no trouble securing a job as a driver on a wagon train headed for California. The route bisected the Great Plains, followed the Platte River for hundreds of miles and crossed the Continental Divide in what became (in 1891) the state of Wyoming. The Continental Divide separates watersheds that drain into the Pacific Ocean from river systems that drain east into the Atlantic Ocean and the Gulf of Mexico. Beyond the Divide, Fisher and the wagon train continued down the Rocky Mountains into the land of Mormon pioneers led by religious leader Brigham Young in what became (in 1896) the state of Utah. The wagon train rolled onward through Nevada and across the Sierra Nevada Mountains into California. They endured skirmishes with hostile American Indian tribes, stampedes of bison through their camp at night and the natural hardships of weather itself (rain, snow, cold). Some members of the wagon train perished and were buried along the trail. Upon arriving in the Golden State after four months and 2,000 miles, Fisher had a surprise encounter—namely, a welcome reunion with his old employer, Uriah Nurse, who was also seeking his fortune in California. Unlike many folks who were testing their abilities as miners in the gold or silver rushes occurring in California and Nevada, Fisher decided against those risks and bet his chances on his newly honed skills as a driver. He chose to drive mule teams pulling wagons loaded with ore from the biggest silver strike in American history, Comstock Lode on the eastern slopes of Mount Davidson (known as Sun Mountain at that time) overlooking Virginia City, Nevada, and hauling the ore over the Sierras to the mill at Marysville, California, a distance of about 150 miles. The mule teams would return to the mine with needed machinery and supplies, then load up ore and go back over the mountains again. It was grueling work crossing over and back with no defined trails, the Sierras often impassable due to heavy snows and dangerous conditions with bandits lurking at strategic locations. Fisher was up to the challenge of the treacherous, demanding job, and the pay was good. The mule teams and drivers were a necessity, without the existence of rail lines, a service four or five years away. Fisher also found work herding horses in the foothills and mountains between Marysville and Oroville. What was the need for horses at that time and place? Well, there were agricultural and ranching ventures in that part of California. Marysville was hailed as the "gateway" for thousands heading to the gold rush sites in California. And there was a stagecoach line running between towns in Northeast California. Horses were definitely needed.

In the fall of 1866, Fisher decided to return home. The journey back turned into another adventure for him. He embarked by steamer through the Golden Gate, a strait connecting San Francisco to the Pacific Ocean, and continued south on an ocean voyage that took him to San Juan del Sur, a Central American port on the west coast of Nicaragua. From there, he walked twenty-five miles to the shores of Lake Nicaragua, catching a steamboat across the lake. Once on the opposite shore, he walked seventy-five miles to the Caribbean Sea. He boarded a freighter in San Juan del Norte (Greytown) bound for New York City. He took a diversion to London, Ontario, likely to visit a friend who was operating a gristmill there. Little did Fisher know how profound that detour would be. This wandering soul found a soul mate, a young woman named Euphemia Robinson. Their meeting was love at first sight, she small (just over five feet tall) and pert, of Irish descent and he tall (well over six feet) and rugged, of Scottish descent. They were married a few months later on July 11, 1867, O.W. almost twenty-five and Euphemia a few months past twenty. He worked at a gristmill for the first few months of their married life in Komoka, Ontario, her birthplace, before they moved back to the States and his home territory, Portsmouth, Ohio, where O.W. gristed flour for a few months. Then they moved back to Ontario, where he operated a mill while simultaneously running a small hotel. In early 1869, the couple, on the move again, landed in Kentucky, where O.W. ran a gristmill that he had worked at a decade earlier and then later a sawmill. Living outside Louisville in a rural area, Euphemia gave birth to their first child on June 5, 1869—a son they named William Peter, in honor of the child's grandfathers.

The young Fishers' transient life continued. In 1871, they moved to Orleans, Missouri, where O.W. purchased and stocked a general store, but that lasted only a short time. Their second son, Andrew James, was born in Orleans on February 7, 1872. Two-year-old William Peter called the baby "Burr," a malapropism of the word *brother*, and the nickname stuck. Years later, Andrew James's name was legally changed to Burr. With a second son, O.W. sold the store, and the Fisher family was on the move again to Kentucky. Having previously purchased forty acres of standing timber, O.W. had secured what he thought was a solid contract to provide wood for the Louisville & Nashville Railroad. The financial scare of 1873 resulted in the contract being canceled. Always keen to respond to what seemed best at the time, O.W. Fisher returned to Orleans, Missouri, repurchased the general

O.W. Fisher and Euphemia Robinson on their wedding day in 1867. *Courtesy of Fisher family.*

store and added another task, that of postmaster. Another son, Oliver David, was born on November 29, 1875. O.W. sold the store in 1877 and acquired a combined sawmill/gristmill in Humansville, Missouri. A fourth son, Daniel Robinson, was born on July 6, 1878. Finally, a daughter, Lula Christina, was born on January 18, 1881. A second daughter, Zoe Edith, was born on May 18, 1884, but died less than three months later. O.W., whose net worth was growing steadily because of his drive and ability, stayed put in Missouri with involvement in various milling and business ventures while his children grew and the family became complete with the birth of Orin Wallace (Wally) on January 8, 1891.

O.W. Fisher had a way about him, a certain aura that attracted people to him and an outward charm that aided him in making alliances that benefited him and others. Fisher developed a long-term friendship with John Briggs Barnett, a go-getter like himself who had served in the Civil War and was a successful mercantile operator, judge and property owner. They gave Humansville its first financial institution, starting the Farmers' and Merchants' Bank. Fisher and Barnett were involved in other profitable ventures. Fisher was an opportunist and visionary. He knew the value of the railroad as virtually the only reliable means of moving people and products. It shaped his decision to push a notion to obtain logs to produce bridge timbers and rail ties for the Fort Scott and Memphis Railroad. There were other meaningful ventures in flour and lumber production but two major endeavors were on the horizon that gave O.W. Fisher the working capital that set him and his family up for their later and lasting

Fisher had its own train at the Louisiana Long Leaf Lumber Company. *The Erickson collection.*

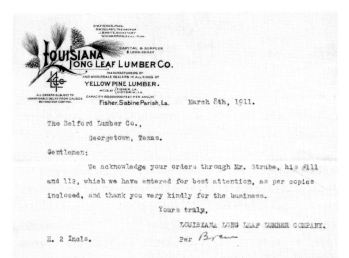

A letter from the Louisiana Long Leaf Lumber Company acknowledges an order from a Texas customer in March 1911. *The Erickson collection.*

The Fisher family poses for a photo (est. 1900). *From left*: Oliver David (O.D.), Burr, Euphemia, Lula Christina, Orin Wallace, William Peter, O.W. and Daniel Robinson. *Courtesy of Fisher family.*

success in the flour business in the Pacific Northwest. They were lumber businesses in Birch Tree, Missouri, and in Fisher, Louisiana, the latter a company town that O.W. Fisher founded and had its own railroad. The Louisiana Long Leaf Lumber Company is long gone, but the town still is in existence today.

MOVING WEST TO MONTANA AND WASHINGTON, O.W. AND HIS CHILDREN EMBARK ON VENTURES

Montana beckoned. Burr and Dan, two sons of O.W. and Euphemia Fisher, had already established a claim, so to speak, moving there to extend their mercantile business, opening stores in Bozeman and Missoula, while Will P. stayed back to run the store in Boulder, Colorado. But after the Boulder store was sold in 1900, Will P. took over the Missoula store, and Dan opened one in Red Lodge, high mountain country some sixty miles from Yellowstone National Park, which was established in 1872 by President Ulysses S. Grant. While his southern lumber investments were flourishing, O.W. Fisher was looking westward for new ventures. He and his son O.D. (Ollie) went on a scouting trip for timberland in 1903 and stopped on the way back to do some fishing in Montana. They visited Burr, who recommended that his father and brother scour the Gallatin Valley, noting that there was a tiny flour mill for sale near Belgrade. O.W. bought the flour mill, and that purchase brought Ollie to Belgrade to manage the mill. O.W. was impressed with the technological improvements, including corrugated steel rolls to crush the wheat and mill the flour. The rolls superseded the buhrstone on which he had learned his miller's trade many decades before. Eventually, O.W. and Euphemia and all of their sons wound up in Montana, and a family home was built in Bozeman. Only their daughter, Lula, remained behind, having gotten married to Willard William Warren, an enterprising young man who succeeded in the management of the Louisiana Long Leaf Lumber (Four L) Company. They continued to live in Fisher, the company town. Will P., O.D. and Burr were married, too. Will P. and his wife, Estelle, had three sons and a daughter. O.D. and his wife, Nellie, had two daughters. Burr and his wife, Jennie, had two sons.

The Fisher family was growing in number, prosperity and prospects. It was 1906, and an earthquake and fire had devastated San Francisco but created an interesting opportunity, one requiring analysis and decisiveness to make a quick move, something for which O.W. Fisher had developed a good business sense over many years. With the Pacific Northwest timberlands on his mind for a while, O.W. entered the Gallatin Valley Milling Company office in Belgrade one morning and asked why his son Ollie was so engrossed in the *Butte Miner*. Ollie replied, as noted by author Herman Steen in his book, *The O.W. Fisher Heritage*, "I'm reading about San Francisco and how progress has been stopped at Van Ness Avenue by dynamiting all the buildings in

The Gallatin Valley Milling Company in Montana became the primary source of grain for the Fisher Flouring Mills on Harbor Island in Seattle. *The Erickson collection.*

a strip a block wide." He continued to explain that he was thinking about the enormous amount of lumber that would be required to rebuild the city and suggested that "this is the time for us to buy as much timber as we can out on the West Coast because prices will move up sharply in the next six months." Steen noted O.W.'s response after pondering the proposition only briefly: "You are undoubtedly right. How soon can you go there and look up some property?" O.D. Fisher quickly took off for western Washington, threw a heavy pack on his back and disappeared in the woods for several weeks on a scouting mission. He came out of the woods to report his findings to a seasoned group of lumbermen, including his father, jointly interested in promising timberlands. The others, all successful and financially solid were E.B. and J.L. Grandin, Captain J.B. White, George and Dan Dulany and W.B. Pettibone. O.D. Fisher urged them to "see for themselves" the opportunities. They did just that and, after their own investigation, made a decision to move on a tract of timber in the Snoqualmie Valley some thirty miles east of Seattle. They immediately organized the Grandin-Coast Lumber Company, named to recognize the Grandin brothers and their keen instinct for moneymaking. O.W. Fisher was elected president of the company, and Ollie was chosen as manager.

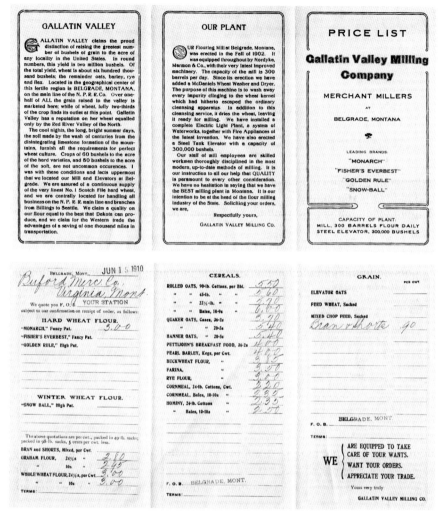

Top: The Gallatin Valley Milling Company in Montana used a brochure promoting its business. *The Erickson collection.*

Bottom: Prices for products listed on the back of a Gallatin Valley Milling Company brochure. *The Erickson collection.*

The Snoqualmie Valley timberland was owned by the Rockefellers, who were willing to sell it because their holdings were in a checkerboard pattern, meaning that sections of the land alternated with property owned by the Weyerhaeuser Timber Company, a Northwest icon. O.D. Fisher had the distinction of informing Weyerhaeuser general manager George

S. Long of the Grandin-Coast group's purchase. The shrewd young Fisher negotiated a deal with Long that had two choices: Weyerhaeuser would sell its timber at the market price to Grandin-Coast when it was ready to be cut or the Weyerhaeuser and Grandin-Coast tracts would be merged and cut by a new company. While this venture was waiting for the timber to be right for harvest, things were happening on other fronts, too. The Fishers weren't letting grass, er, trees grow under their collective feet. There were opportunities to be had in Seattle, a city in the midst of growing pains, ready to burst into its own with immense potential through shipping, fisheries and lumbering. The most dominant business entity in Seattle at the time was the Alaska Building, and the entire business district was on Second Avenue near that structure. The city's hills were being pared down as more than 30 billion yards of dirt were moved, largely by hydraulic action, to build up the tideflats for a Seattle industrial area and later to create a man-made island called Harbor Island to facilitate ships delivering goods from around the world and hauling products bound for Europe, South

The Fisher Company purchased timberland in the Snoqualmie Valley from the Rockefellers in 1906 and forged a partnership with Weyerhaeuser to operate what became the Snoqualmie Falls Lumber Company. *The Erickson collection.*

32

America and Asia. Transcontinental rail service allowed large quantities of goods to move across Seattle's docks. Hills not yet touched for their fill dirt were still the domain of Jersey cows grazing peacefully. The Fishers, with considerable wealth by this time, were ready to forge ahead, and they were connected with associates who had even more funds at their disposal. Will P. Fisher was proprietor of the Fisher Trading Company, a flour brokerage business. O.D. Fisher invested in the Metropolitan Building Company, which had fifty-year leases on downtown Seattle lots that were part of an endowment of the University of Washington and was beginning to erect and operate office buildings on those grounds. But in 1909, the largest step of all was about to be taken.

PART II

BUILDING:
FISHER EMPIRE STARTS ITS RISE

FISHER FLOURING MILLS FOUNDED, SCONES LAUNCHED, NEWTON COLEMAN KEY PROMOTER

Seattle was booming, and the Fisher family was prospering along with the city's economic growth. The Fishers were always watchful for any new opportunities. One day in April 1909, O.W. Fisher and his son O.D. Fisher were crossing Second Avenue at Yesler Way in downtown Seattle. The father stopped suddenly, and the abrupt action made his son come to a halt as well, halfway across the intersection. Luckily, there was no traffic headed their way. O.W. excitedly exclaimed to his son, as they viewed Elliott Bay and Harbor Island created in the bay from dirt taken off the city's hills, "Look at all the ships in the harbor." He suggested the island would be a good place to build a flour milling plant because their company would be able to ship flour all over the world. Reportedly, the pair found a rowboat on the dock and borrowed it to circumnavigate the island to determine the best possible location. Three months later, the Fisher Flouring Mills Company was formed and the decision made to move forward on building the plant. A contract was let to the Nordyke & Marmon Company, recognized as the leading builder of flour mills in the United States. Construction began in the fall of 1910, was finished by spring of 1911 and the first wheat ground in mid-April. The mills officially opened for business in June, when the first flour was sold. So it was that a father and son were instrumental in founding a two-unit facility, representing an investment of $400,000 (more than $12 million in today's dollars). Equipped to grind about ten thousand bushels of wheat a day, the plant had a capacity to create two thousand barrels of flour a day. Although the Fisher family believed their flour to be the best there was, little did they know it was better than what was officially considered the best. The *Seattle Star* newspaper reported in May 1912 that, without the Fisher Company's knowledge, the Columbus Laboratories of Chicago tested Fisher's Blend flour for a North Dakota wheat grower and found Fisher's Blend flour higher in quality, gluten content, water absorption and general value than the best Dakota all-hard wheat flour that was recognized as the industry standard. The newspaper noted that Fisher's Blend flour was a combination of eastern hard wheat and western soft wheat, which preserved the best qualities of each and cost about 25 percent less than a straight eastern hard-wheat flour. How to best promote its Blend brand flour? The Fisher family reached back into its Scotch ancestry and decided it would be relatively easy to make scones and give them away or sell them for a nickel.

Above and following two pages: The exterior and interior work to create the Fisher Flouring Mills on Harbor Island took less than a year to build, and the mills were open for business by the middle of 1911. *Photos courtesy of A.J. Milliken collection.*

The completed Fisher Flouring Mills was strategically situated on Harbor Island to accommodate ships transporting its flour and feed to West Coast ports. *Courtesy of University of Washington collection.*

The Fishers also turned to an enterprising African American, Newton Coleman, to be the key spokesman for the Blend flour and the image on flour bags and advertising material. Coleman's first major appearance was heading the Fisher scones booth at the Panama-Pacific International Exposition in 1915 in San Francisco, where he introduced Fisher's Blend flour and Fisher scones to millions of visitors. Known as "Blend" for advertising promotions to pitch Fisher's Blend flour, Coleman followed up his starring role at that landmark world's fair by appearing at many fairs and events up and down the West Coast. Sometimes, he got newspaper coverage. For instance, in early March 1916, the *Oregon Daily Journal* noted that Coleman would be at Portland's Meier & Frank store making and selling Fisher scones at the store's Pure Food exhibit and that "Blend" would interest people "with his kindly humor and short sermons" on the merits of Fisher's Blend flour and orders for the flour would be taken at the food booth. The *Tacoma Times* reported on March 23, 1916, that Coleman would be at McCormick Brothers' store for a week making scones and selling each one, along with the scone recipe, for five cents. Coleman explained to the newspaper and folks coming to the store that more than 2 million Fisher scones were sold at the exposition, and people wanted the recipe. But the recipe was kept secret, for months, he noted, and finally given to the public only after more than 100,000 people had asked for it. Coleman had high praise for his scones, confidently boasting to all who would listen that Fisher scones were the "greatest bits of pastry known to the culinary art." While Coleman's schedule would not allow him to

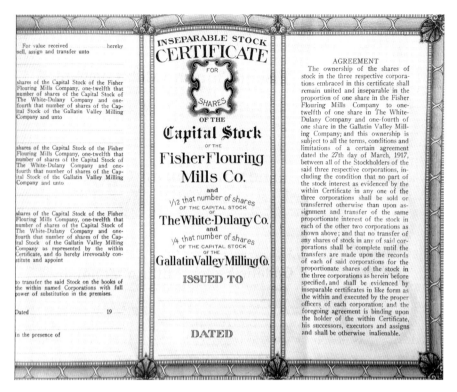

The Fisher Flouring Mills Company offered stock for interested investors. *Courtesy A.J. Milliken collection.*

be at every West Coast store, some places would do promotions using a photo of Coleman at the San Francisco exposition and the descriptive phrasing, "Blend making SCONES the by-word of the exposition." For example, as noted in an advertisement in the *Tulare Advance-Register*, located in Tulare, California, on March 24, 1916, the Tulare Rochdale Company stated that if a customer would purchase a bag of Fisher's Blend flour, the company would "thereupon mail direct a nice calendar hanger with the Fisher Scone recipe printed in full." Follow the instructions, the company exclaimed, and "you'll have no trouble turning out this delicious morsel, just the thing for special luncheons and teas." Coleman continued to be the front man for Fisher's flour and scones, appearing at many locations each year. The *Tacoma Daily Ledger* reported on September 12, 1920, that Coleman would be at Standard House Furnishing Company in downtown Tacoma for a week baking scones and rolls from Fisher's Blend flour in a "big window demonstration" using a Monarch "perfect" oven, which was among the line of products the company sold.

This all led to the topper of road trips. In 1919, the Fisher Flouring Mills had a food truck, a vehicle built by the Dodge auto company. The milling company began using it from late July to late fall of that year, touring Washington, Oregon and Idaho, stopping at all the county, state and community fairs on the way. At every stop, Coleman, now truly a famous chef, turned out his tasty products and distributed them to anxious and interested onlookers. The *Seattle Daily Times* on July 27, 1919, reported that the trip of the Dodge food truck, so far as was known, was the first of its kind ever attempted in the Northwest. The vehicle was equipped with a special electric oven that had the necessary fixtures for attaching it to the circuits of any power line in America so Fisher scones and biscuits could be prepared wherever it went. Fisher's advertising display manager H.W. Bryan was in charge of the venture. But everyone knew that Blend (Coleman) was the real star. The Seattle newspaper stated that "automobile men of Seattle looked upon the feat of the Fisher Flouring Mills as indicative of what may be accomplished along lines of demonstration with an automobile." The *Tacoma Daily Ledger* reported on September 28, 1919, that Fisher's use of a "fine, speedy, and reliable motor car was responsible for a new way of advertising to get in direct contact with the market." Termed an "automobile" or "car" in the news articles, the vehicle really resembled a delivery truck of that

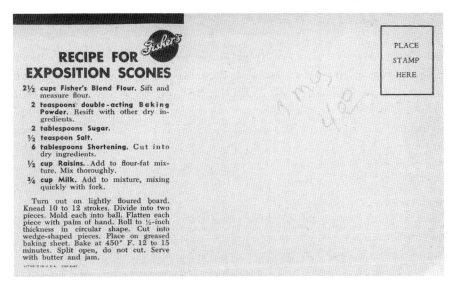

The official Fisher scone recipe was a secret until so many people requested it that the Fisher Company relented and released it. Raisins were in the recipe until the early 1970s. *The Erickson collection.*

era. Whatever! So confident of its potential, Fisher Mills ordered a similar electric oven vehicle, even before its first vehicle had finished its road trip. Fisher Mills officials indicated they chose Dodge vehicles because they were "best suited to the heavy road work expected on demonstration trips." Fisher Mills, ever inventive, was rolling along, ahead of the game in its effort to bring Fisher Flour and its products to the public.

FISHER SCONES HAILED AT 1915 EXPO

Fisher Flouring Mills on man-made Harbor Island in Seattle was slowly gaining respect after opening for business in 1911, making and selling scones filled with butter, raspberry jam and raisins to promote sales of its flour. It wasn't until 1915, however, that Fisher scones got the attention of the entire planet thanks to their presence at a world's fair, officially called the Panama-Pacific International Exposition, a celebration marking the completion of the Panama Canal and the rise of host city San Francisco from the ruins of the catastrophic 1906 earthquake and fire.

For nine months, an electric atmosphere existed as nearly 19 million visitors came to the West Coast of America for this momentous gathering. The exposition galvanized the world into frenzied action to revolutionize trade between countries of Europe and Asia since the Panama Canal was a gateway connecting the Atlantic and Pacific Oceans for faster and easier transport of goods to marketplaces.

While Fisher scones didn't become a worldwide commodity as a result of the fair's exposure, they did become a popular delicacy in their homeland, the Pacific Northwest. William Paulhamus, a founder of the fair in Puyallup, Washington, attended the exposition with his young son, Dwight, and saw long lines of people waiting to be served at the Fisher's Blend booth in the Palace of Food Products. He recalled that "jam on hot biscuits" were being handed out by a tall man in a chef's uniform. Back home, Paulhamus contacted the Fisher family and obtained an agreement to have Fisher scones sold at the 1915 Puyallup Fair, with a promise from the fair founder to provide the jam free of charge.

A period newspaper article, reprinted in the *Seattle Times*, praised the Fisher scones sold at the exposition, calling them "the most popular product sold in the Food Products building. The famous Fisher's Blend scones were made and sold to the eager throngs that constantly surrounded the booth.

Left: Euphemia Fisher (*second from left*) and family and Fisher Company representatives, particularly Newton Coleman (*far right*), were at the Panama-Pacific Exposition in San Francisco in 1915 to sell Fisher scones and promote Fisher's Blend flour. *Courtesy Calisphere, University of California collection.*

Below: Newton Coleman (*right center*) headed the baking demonstration at the Fisher Scone booth at the 1915 Panama-Pacific Exposition in San Francisco. *Courtesy Calisphere, University of California collection.*

As many as twenty-five thousand of these scones were baked and sold in a single day and during the life of the exposition more than two million were turned out." This was followed by a positive critique: "When served hot, with raspberry jam between two layers, these scones were a most palatable morsel of food." And the cost? Five cents per scone.

That was a pretty heady endorsement, considering there were others selling scones at their respective booths. Most prominent, however, was the Sperry Flour Company, which devoted its effort almost entirely to the "Bread of All Nations" theme with scones as an afterthought. Sperry's "Bread" exhibit had a multitude of tiny kitchens in which cooks from many nations, in costume, were at work demonstrating some special preparations of their homelands for which Sperry flour was a main ingredient. Russians offered Petosky meat rolls, *aladdi, careniki, perbaly babka* and *kasha*. Scandinavians, in bright apparel, offered *olands brod* and *mannagryns kaka*. French cooks offered doughnuts and croissants. Chinese offered fried seed cakes. Hindu *pakauvi* was made by a native of India. Hebrew noodle pudding, Japanese tea cakes and Mexican enchiladas could also be found. Visitors left with not only samples but also recipes. The Sperry exhibit included a three-story mill and a Marshall continuous oven. The Fisher exhibit employed a Marshall double oven to bake its scones.

Writer/author Laura Ingalls Wilder, of *Little House on the Prairie* fame, traveled by train from her farm home in Missouri to visit her daughter, Rose Wilder Lane, in San Francisco and took in the exposition. Ingalls Wilder relished strolling through the food products building and getting a taste literally of all that was offered. She enjoyed the "breads from different nations" but particularly loved the scones. It is not clear whether she targeted her approval directly to Fisher scones, but one might draw that connection since all the scones at the exposition were prepared similarly in the tradition of Scotch scones.

After she had returned home, Ingalls Wilder wrote an article, "Magic in Plain Foods," for the *Missouri Ruralist* in which she noted, "I am sure nobody leaves the exposition without speaking of the Scotch scones. Everybody eats them who can reach them. They are baked by a Scotchman from Edinburgh, who turns out more that 4,000 of them daily. They are buttered, spread with jam, and handed over the counter as fast as four girls can do it. And the counter is surrounded by a surging mob all day long."

On a postcard to her father, Almanzo Wilder, Rose Wilder Lane offered this commentary about her mother, taking advantage of food so readily available from a city by an ocean or offered at this one-of-a-kind exposition:

"Mama is growing fat. I don't know whether or not it is the fish she eats. She eats a tremendous amount of it. Perhaps, it is the Scotch scones. They are very delicious, crumbly, hot cakes, spread thick with butter and jam. She eats two of them without a quiver. Once she ate three." That revelation appeared in a well-researched book, *Rose Wilder Lane's San Francisco*, by Trini L. Wenninger. What's important is that the famous author of *Little House on the Prairie* brought back scones she loved to the prairie she loved.

HOUSEHOLDS DEMANDED FISHER'S BLEND FLOUR

During the early years of the Fisher Flouring Mills operation, the major production was flour for the household trade. The emphasis was on promotion of Fisher's Blend flour for use by families, and an enterprising African American named Newton Coleman was the baker and spokesman at many activities at grocery stores, fairs and other venues throughout Washington and Oregon. That included road trips in 1919 and 1920 in a specially made food truck that took Fisher scones to the people where they were, in order to sell the company's flour. Times were changing, and the children of O.W. and Euphemia Fisher were exerting their force within the

Even O.D. Fisher, who became president of the company and Fisher Mills manager after the death of his father, O.W., in 1922, had to carry a company ID card. *Courtesy A.J. Milliken collection.*

company. O.W. was mourning the loss of his wife, who died on March 2, 1921, and then he was hit with another blow when his son-in-law Willard Warren died less than six weeks later. Warren, manager of the Snoquamie Valley Lumber Company, was beloved by employees there. O.W. was greatly affected by both losses, and his health declined. He died on June 22, 1922, three months shy of what would have been his eightieth birthday. Finally, Newton Coleman died on October 12, 1922, at the age of sixty-five, after a lingering illness.

Newton Coleman was the man people saw in person, pitching Fisher's Blend flour and Fisher scones, as well as its recipe. He was called "Blend." His face was on the bags of flours and other promotional material, including the Fisher cookbooks of the 1930s and newspaper advertisements. An obituary in the *Seattle Star* on October 13, 1922, stated that Newton Coleman was a person "most widely known in the Pacific Northwest." The short obit noted that Coleman died at his residence, 1813 Twenty-Fourth Avenue, and that a funeral was to be held two days hence at Mount Zion Baptist Church, Nineteenth Avenue and Madison. The only other information pertinent to his life was a reference to him being born into slavery in Kentucky. No mention of his association with the Fisher Flouring Mills or scones. But the newspaper declared he was "widely known." For what? Fisher Flour and Fisher scones, that's what. Everyone who bought flour or read newspaper ads knew. His face was used for promotional purposes throughout the 1920s and 1930s. Then it was gone. Did the Fisher Flouring Mills retire his image out of respect for someone who served the company well and was no longer alive? I'd like to think so. But I was unable to get confirmation from anyone representing the Fisher Company or any written document or journal. I contacted the Northwest African-American Museum and the Black Heritage Society of Washington Museum, both in Seattle, and was told that neither had any information on Newton Coleman. On my own, I searched and found that Newton Coleman is buried in Seattle's Lakeview Cemetery.

Newton Coleman, noted front man for Fisher scones and Fisher's Blend flour, died in 1922 and is buried in Seattle's Lakeview Cemetery, where many Seattle pioneers and celebrities have been laid to rest. *Photo by Keith Erickson.*

The Hillsdale Store, located at East Sixty-Fourth and McKinley in Tacoma, had a Fisher's Blend advertising sign painted on its outside wall during the 1920s. *The Erickson collection.*

The August Suderburg Store in the town of Alder, on the road to Mount Rainier, had a Fisher advertising sign on its outside wall to lure customers inside about 1930. The site where this store stood is now underwater, part of the Alder Lake reservoir. *Courtesy of the Carl Linden collection.*

Fisher Flour sold well among families in the 1930s, and demand from bakeries in Washington and Oregon grew, eventually overtaking sales directly to households. But California became the boom market, as bakeries discovered and loved Fisher Flour for use in making pastries, cakes, cookies and other tasty treats for their customers. The popularity for Fisher Flour continued into the 1940s, despite lost opportunities to fully promote it

You can still find a Fisher advertising sign on a wall if you go look for it in downtown Puyallup, but you have a better view if you wait until all the fall leaves are gone from the trees. *Photo by Keith Erickson.*

because all of the fairs, which people were accustomed to attending, were shut down for three years during World War II. The Fisher Company had its advertising message painted on the sides of stores and barns all over Washington State, sort of a forerunner of today's billboards alongside highways. There is even one bridge in southwest Washington where the faded artwork is somewhat visible if you get up close and personal. A newer, more vibrant Fisher's Blend painting stands out on the side of a building in downtown Puyallup.

SWEET SCONES MESH WITH SCENTS IN HAWAII

When Mr. and Mrs. H.W. Bryan of Seattle's Fisher Flouring Mills stepped off a ship in the harbor of Honolulu on a September day in 1924, they couldn't help but be overwhelmed by the fragrance carried on the light tropical breeze. A hypnotic elixir was created by the combining force of multiple flowers releasing their scents for all to enjoy: plumeria, ginger, jasmine, naupaka, tuberose, gardenia, orchid, crinum lily, mock orange, maile. The Bryans were determined to add to the seemingly never-ending sweetness that hung in the air. They did just that. The delicious scent of Fisher scones blended with the intoxicating aroma of the Hawaiian Islands, and the result was the sweet smell of success at the Territorial and Maui fairs. As Fisher's advertising director, Bryan was instrumental in promoting the company's blended flour, instant oats cereal and dairy and poultry feeds.

He set up exhibits, with assistance from staff from Theo H. Davis & Company, Limited, local distribution agent for the Fisher Flouring Mills. Besides the exhibits of products, there were baking demonstrations of cakes, biscuits and the famous Fisher scones, popularized by the 1915 exposition in San Francisco. Bryan always advocated for such demonstrations because of their value, showing people the high quality of the blended flour used for baking. The Bryans brought four electric ovens with them to Hawaii to facilitate the demonstrations. Mrs. Bryan handled the free distribution of Fisher scones, with butter and sweet raspberry jam. The scones proved very popular, as raspberries and jam made from that fruit were a rarity on the islands.

Besides the work of the fair, the Bryans created window and display exhibits promoting Fisher products at local stores using their expertise gained from being in charge of such store and fair exhibits and demonstrations throughout Washington, Oregon and California. The Bryans also were instrumental in bringing William Coats, head of the Fisher Flouring Mills feed department, to take responsibility for running the feed exhibits and judging poultry entries at the Territorial and Maui fairs. The Fisher scones were such a hit, the Bryans stayed for another month or so promoting Fisher products and establishing a merchandising foothold on the islands. For instance, they created enormous interest by staging a baking contest at a Theo H. Davis grocery store. The contest drew more than five hundred entries. All day long, people wound their way through the doors of the store, showed their receipt that they had purchased the famous Fisher's Blend flour for baking purposes and left their item. Pancakes, biscuits, cakes, pies, loaves of bread and other pastry items overflowed on tables set up to display the products. Three local judges, watching the marching bakers, were aghast at what appeared to be such quality products assembled and knew their job would be extremely difficult. Winning entrants won prizes, but there was another big winner, too. The culinary items were auctioned off, and the proceeds benefited the Shriners' Hospital fund. A fun time was had by all, and the Aloha Temple band provided musical support for the event. There were many comments from purchasers that they couldn't believe they could get such quality products. It proved there were many good bakers on the islands and that the Fisher's Blend flour was a success in their recipes. Bryan, who said he had conducted many such baking demonstrations and contests, had high praise for the islanders' effort, admitting, "I've never seen a better one." Several days after the baking contest, the Bryans sailed back to their home in Seattle with good memories. Despite their busy days, they found time to develop friendships with folks who regretted the Bryans' departure.

Those friends were so happy, however, when the next year, in September 1925, the Bryans returned. They extended an amazed greeting as the Bryans disembarked from a ship in the harbor. People couldn't wait for the cry, "Right this way, piping hot," that they knew would greet them at the scone booths. And the scones, they said, were just as good as ever. Besides the scone booths, the Fisher Company had poultry and livestock booths displaying their feed products. Again, William Coats of the company's feed department was on hand to lend his knowledgeable judging touch to the poultry competition. Upon arrival, Bryan had nice things to say about the 1924 fairs that encouraged him to come back, telling fair officials: "We were well pleased with our demonstrations at the fairs and the publicity work done here last year. We returned home to Seattle full of enthusiasm for your fair and have been spreading that enthusiasm all over the Pacific Northwest. The people of Hawaii sure made a booster out of us for the fairs and the Islands." Bryan urged Hawaiians to keep their fairs going because of their invaluable importance, saying, "I would like to impress on the good people of these wonderful islands what assets good fairs are to them. Get behind your fairs and put them over big and you will be repaid in many ways." The Territorial and Maui Fairs featured a unique demonstration this time around, one showing how everyone the world over could use Fisher's Blend flour. Throughout the fairs, there would be four demonstrations: a Chinese woman in native costume showing how she uses the flour in baking her ethnic dishes, a Japanese woman in a bright-colored kimono baking the pastries and breads of Japan, a Portuguese woman showcasing her country's delicacies and an American woman demonstrating use of flour in U.S. products. Knowing the value of effective displays, Bryan arranged a striking display of sacks of flour along with beautiful sheaves of wheat from which the flour is made. Set against a backdrop of black satin, the exhibit turned heads, causing memorable reactions from fairgoers. The Bryans left Hawaii with warm feelings toward the Islanders and happy to create a market for the Fisher's Blend flour for many years to come.

Creating a Distribution Network

How did Fisher's products go from mill to consumer? There were several methods of travel. Boat: an image from the 1950s shows a vessel, *Burrard*, docked at the Fisher Flour Mills pier on Harbor Island. Rail: several warehouses, Bellingham, Tacoma, Portland, had tracks laid or alongside to connect to other parts of the country. Truck: when warehouse locations shifted to a new area in the same city, loading docks were constructed at the new sites to haul in large quantities of flour; a permit variance is on file for such in Portland.

The completion of their massive mill operation on Harbor Island in 1911 required agents along the West Coast to sell and promote the various lines of Fisher products, from graham flour to poultry feed, and the storage to accommodate. The publications put out by Fisher Flour over the years hint at an expansion and then concentration on what they deemed as key markets. Listed on the back cover of *The Fairies Cookbook*, October 1924, are locations with principal offices or agents: Seattle, Tacoma, Bellingham, Mount Vernon, Portland, San Francisco, Los Angeles, San Diego, Hong Kong, New York. A 1941 edition of the *Fisher's Blend Baking Book* tallies only Tacoma, Portland, San Francisco and Los Angeles in addition to headquarters in Seattle.

Almost immediately Fisher rented space in the Merchants Exchange Building, one of the few buildings to survive the 1906 San Francisco earthquake and subsequent fires. This presence helped them logistically when they displayed their foods at the 1915 Panama-Pacific International Exposition. For over half a century, Fisher maintained an office and warehouse in the Bay Area. The first person of contact for the San Francisco branch was a member of the Fisher family, Burr, who had moved to the Bay Area from Montana where he had run a mercantile business and later managed the Gallatin Valley Flour Mill. He stayed in San Francisco for many years. Burr's brother Dan, who also had operated a mercantile store in Montana, took over as manager of Gallatin, where he remained for some time. Gallatin was the key supplier of grain for the Fisher Flouring Mills.

Burr handed off day-to-day duties to William J. McElroy. He was their manager for over twenty-five years. During this period, the Fisher Flour San Francisco sales department moved from room 618 of the Merchants Exchange Building to a spot inside its warehouse, 568 Seventh Street, a building that exists in some form today. After the Second World War, Fisher

The Gallatin Valley Milling Company no longer exists, but an abandoned grain elevator bearing its name still stands tall near Bozeman, Montana. *Photo by Keith Erickson.*

Feed stores had temperature signs provided by the Fisher Company to market products. *Courtesy of A.J. Milliken collection.*

Flour transported goods in and out of a warehouse at 1566 Carroll Avenue, and A.L. Clark and subsequently W. Alan Bonner served as persons of contact for the company until 1968, when Fisher Flour executives decided to begin winding down the entire enterprise.

Another nascent Fisher Flour market was Tacoma. The company established a presence in the City of Destiny in 1912, setting up shop in the warehouse district, presently occupied by the University of Washington–Tacoma. Two managers, John Featherstone and Hubert Squibb, oversaw the early years, as they rented space in nearby buildings, 1919 Commerce and 1840 and 1920 Pacific Avenue, along the Prairie Line, a Northern Pacific Railroad spur, on an annual contract. In 1915, Fisher decided to let Pacific

Workers pose for a picture at Fisher Mills' Tacoma distribution center a century ago, one of its many West Coast warehouses at that time. *Courtesy Northwest Room, Tacoma Public Library.*

Sacks of Fisher flour are being loaded onto the freighter *Hactum* in June 1920, at the Tacoma wharf. The ship was bound for Europe, with its first stop in Liverpool. *Courtesy Northwest Room, Tacoma Public Library.*

Storage and Transfer, 1721 Jefferson, act as its agents while it searched for a more permanent arrangement.

"An announcement of importance to the people of Tacoma and Pierce County" is the lead sentence of an article in the *Tacoma Daily Ledger* from December 15, 1918, and reads more like an advertisement: "Fisher Flouring Mills Company Acquires International Fisheries Dock...Headquarters is now in Tacoma." The article paints a picture of the "largest milling concern west of Minneapolis, with a capacity of 6,000 barrels of flour a day....Beginning tomorrow the company's various milling products will be on sale at leading Tacoma stores." It speaks glowingly about the reputation of Fisher's hog, pig and dog feed. Fisher hired H.B. Clark and T. Drumm of John B. Stevens Company to be manager and assistant manager, respectively. Fisher Flour now has a Tacoma site necessary to move and store its goods, 1002 East D Street. In 1922, Godfrey E. Madsen assumed managerial duties. He stayed until 1932, when Fisher decided to move into a location on the west side of the city currently known as Thea Foss Waterway. Robert H. Stewart oversaw a decade of day-to-day operations at 1153 Dock. Ray Holt followed. The closing years of Fisher Flour in Tacoma were governed by Elmer Miller, shipping clerk and foreman. By 1970, Fisher Flour had ceased to have a branch in Tacoma.

Fisher Flouring Mills conducted commerce in the Los Angeles area for many years out of a facility in Vernon, 4255 Produce Plaza. Other businesses shared the same structure.

The first Portland Fisher Flour warehouse was at 247 Union, presently known as Martin Luther King Jr. Boulevard. A railroad spur extended to the loading area. The last warehouse located in the Rose City was a one-and-a-half-story building, 307 Southeast Washington. Flour and feed were hauled by truck. Offices were upstairs. Records indicate supervisors of the remaining days of Fisher Flour as Frances Dayton; R.M. Abrams, a transfer from Bellingham; and ultimately Raymond Ryland.

AUTHOR'S NOTE: *My son Keith Erickson compiled research and wrote this piece on Fisher's distribution network.*

PART III
EVOLVING:
OUTREACH TACTICS SWITCHED

SHE WAS A BAKING QUEEN IN THE 1930S

A humble, unassuming woman shrugged off her shyness and became an assertive force for "flour power" as the first Mary Mills in the early 1930s, promoting Fisher Fair Scones, and ultimately Seattle's Fisher Flouring Mills. That's the story Suzanne Hall tells of her mother, who loved scones and passed on that love to others, including Hall. "Her name was already Mary, so it was easy to take the Mary Mills stage name," said Hall, who was born on October 4, 1938, after her mother had given up the pitchwoman job and gotten married. Her mother, whose maiden name was Gregory, traced her ancestry back to the *Mayflower* and a family named Fuller. That kind of determination and grit to do such research in an age without the internet was something Mary Gregory carried through her life from her early beginnings when she majored in home economics at the University of Washington. She became a registered dietitian at a time when there were few dietitians anywhere and, consequently, few jobs in the field. After graduation, she went to Chicago for an internship that had her parents worried. The Windy City was a place of high crime, and there was the influence of the Mob led by the legendary Al Capone. She had already established herself as an independent woman bent on doing her own thing, rejecting the pleas of her father, J.C. Gregory, to study journalism and join his newspaper, the *Bothel Sentinel*. She boldly moved forward.

Left: Suzanne Hall, daughter of the first Mary Mills who promoted Fisher's flour, talked about her life and her mother's life during an interview in early 2022. *Photo by Keith Erickson.*

Right: Mary Gregory, a University of Washington graduate, became Mary Mills in the early 1930s. *Courtesy of Suzanne Hall family.*

When Mary Gregory unpacked her clothes before assuming her internship as a dietitian at a hospital, she removed from her bags a small pistol she had brought to protect herself while residing in a tough Chicago neighborhood and walking to the nearby hospital. Her job was preparing meals for patients in the facility. Did she run into the noted gangster? "I asked my mother if she met Al Capone," Hall recounted, "and she said she did. She explained that Capone's wife was there having a baby and that Capone had a room down the hall from his wife. She said she took meals down to him, and, of course, to his wife." Meeting Al Capone? Really? "Yes, really, my mother told me," Hall recalled. "And my mother was never known to tell a lie. So, it had to be true. I believe it." It certainly was a good story.

NOTE: *According to Chicago newspapers, Al Capone and his wife, Mae, had a son in 1918 but were unable to have any other children. Mae ended several subsequent pregnancies with either stillbirths or miscarriages. So, in 1930, it's possible that Mae was at Michael Reese Hospital during one of those medical situations while Gregory was working there.*

Later, Gregory was offered a job at an orphanage for $175 a month (good money back then), plus room and board and uniforms. She called her father, who, still concerned about her safety, urged her to come home. She heeded his advice and did return. While jobs were scarce, University of Washington professors helped her connect with a lunchroom run by wealthy women to benefit what was then Children's Orthopedic Hospital in Seattle. Because much of the food was donated, developing a menu was a challenge. One had to get creative. It was a job suited to Gregory's talent. Gregory's effort eventually caught the attention of one wealthy woman whose curiosity was punctuated by continual questions. Then, one day, Gregory received a message from the woman's husband, asking that she come to his office at Fisher Flouring Mills on Harbor Island.

A chauffeur (Gregory in her journal used the word *messenger*) picked up Gregory and drove her to the mills, where she met Wallace "Wally" Fisher. He sent her home with flour and instructions to bake a butter cake and an angel food cake. She was told to bring the unfrosted cakes back the next day. Again, someone picked up Gregory, along with her creations, and drove to the mills. Hall said her mother remembered that a "bunch of men sat around a table and picked the cakes apart" literally and figuratively to evaluate the texture and taste. A few days later, Hall said, her mother got a call from Wally Fisher, who declared that she, Mary Gregory, was going to be Mary Mills. By 1932, milling techniques had changed; there were better flours, and recipes from cookbooks two decades earlier needed to be updated. Furthermore, the gigantic recipe to accommodate thousands of customers at Washington fairs, where scones had become a tradition for more than fifteen years, had to be pared down to a box-size mix for bakers at home. No way would home cooks have a need for recipes requiring a fifty-pound sack of flour or a whole can of shortening.

Fisher's Mary Mills was important to the flour making company. She tested the recipes by baking the dishes—a long, but rewarding process— and revamped the Fisher Mills cookbooks. She also reworked the fair scone recipe in order to develop the popular home baking mix. All the recipes at that time (during the 1930s, the Depression era) used milk with the Blend flour mix. As Mary Mills, she was featured in newspaper articles and advertisements. She also had a call-in radio show on KOMO Radio, a station created by the Fisher family in 1926, primarily to promote their Blend flour. Mary Mills also made public appearances to promote Fisher's flour, and often scones were given away to people attending the events.

Above: The *Fisher's Cooky Book* was marketed to households in the 1930s to persuade them to make recipes using Fisher's Blend flour. *The Erickson collection.*

Right: Fisher promoted Mary Gregory as Mary Mills in a *Tacoma Daily Ledger* advertisement. *Northwest Room, Tacoma Public Library.*

Sometimes at such events, like grocery store grand openings, customers could purchase the scone recipe for a nickel and get a scone for free. Mary Mills worked closely with Fisher's advertising manager, Rudy Oser. They fell in love and married. Mary Mills hung up her Fisher apron, retired and became a homemaker, Mary Gregory Oser. There were other Mary Mills who followed in her footsteps. Suzanne Hall said she was born in 1938 and remembers her mother being a wonderful cook and baker. No surprise there. Rudy Oser died about 1960, and Mary Oser went back to work as a dietitian at Providence Hospital. She remarried, becoming Mary Oser Biles. Suzanne Hall said her mother, who had a knack for preparing food, "loved to tell people that she had been Mary Mills promoting scones

The original 1932

THE SEATT

NO EASY TASK THIS!

Dorothy Neighbors, right, and Mary Mills, home economics expert for the Fisher Flouring Mills Company, had a big job on their hands yesterday when they began arranging the cakes entered in Dorothy Neighbors Cake Baking Contest, sponsored by the Fisher Flouring Mills Company, in numerical order so that they might be returned to their owners today. The prize awards were to be made this afternoon in the fifth floor auditorium of Rhodes Department Store at Dorothy's special cake baking demonstration.

Mary Mills joined Dorothy Neighbors for a baking demonstration. *Courtesy of Suzanne Hall family.*

Mary Oser Biles liked to recall her days as the first Mary Mills, updating Fisher cookbooks. *Courtesy of Suzanne Hall family.*

and Fisher flour." Did her mother's legacy rub off on Hall? "I've cooked for big family gatherings," Hall said, "and people told me I was good at it, but it was just something I did. Not as much passion as my mom." Except when Hall went above and beyond after her mother died in 2007 at the age of ninety-nine. In a true act of love, Hall made scones for those attending the funeral of her mother. What a tasteful tribute.

Hall doesn't bake much these days. Her husband, Tom, who worked in construction, died in 2014. She lives by herself in Redmond. Her children have their own lives: Todd, a salesman for Frito-Lay; Darren, a mechanic and former auto racer; Matthew, who is disabled; and Melissa, a bookkeeper. Suzanne Hall has sweet memories, however, of the tasty delicacies her mother made, and that's enough to satisfy her.

AUTHOR'S NOTE: *I interviewed Suzanne Hall on January 26, 2022, for this book, and she died on March 22, 2022, of heart failure, after visiting one of her favorite places, the University of Washington campus in Seattle, to enjoy the trees full of beautiful cherry blossoms. I was determined to attend her Party for Life and, like she did for her mother, bring Fisher scones to share. I did just that for her party on May 15, 2022. Suzanne Hall was a remarkable person I learned from comments by family and friends: She was full of a generous spirit, which she extended, along with a welcoming attitude, to everyone she knew. She had been an elementary school teacher, had tutored children and had marketed various products, including Princess House crystal, Mary Kay cosmetics, and World Book encyclopedias. She had a passion for sewing, creating dresses and costumes for family members. She enjoyed decorating cakes for the parties she loved to host and encouraged family and friends to take cake baking classes. In her artistic endeavors, Suzanne certainly made her mother and others proud. I have chosen to leave her story intact as if she were alive, because she is, you know, in the hearts of so many people she touched.*

FISHER MILLS A CREDIT TO NW AND AMERICA

By the 1930s, the Fisher Flouring Mills Company was gaining a reputation as one of the outstanding industries in the Pacific Northwest. Its mills on Harbor Island was the largest facility west of the Mississippi River and recognized as America's "finest flouring mills." A leading expert even said so, and that endorsement and other information about Fisher's products was reported in the April 10, 1934 edition of the *Bellingham (WA) Herald*. The expert cited in the newspaper article was L.I. Ziegler, chief milling engineer for George Urban Milling Company of Buffalo, New York, noted for its Liberty Flour. Ziegler's reputation and skills were noted because of his engineering involvement in more than 1,200 milling plants. Those facilities were located throughout the United States, Canada, Mexico, Central America, South America, China, Japan and Russia. The newspaper reported that Ziegler hailed the Fisher Flouring Mills as "more extensively equipped than any of the milling plants with which I have anything to do in an engineering way."

The newspaper maintained that was an astounding compliment by a man "who occupied a position comparable to that of Mr. Steinmetz in the electrical world." That made Ziegler's assessment even more incredible, considering that the reference was to Charles Proteus Steinmetz, an electrical engineer labeled a genius in mathematics and electronics, a man with more than two hundred patents. Steinmetz fostered the development of alternating current that made possible the expansion of the electrical power industry in the United States. He formulated mathematical theories for engineers and made groundbreaking discoveries that enabled engineers to design better electromagnetic apparatus equipment, especially electric motors for use in industry.

Ziegler based his opinion on facts that the Fisher Mills was operating its "many departments in orderly fashion with highly trained workers." The newspaper reported the following facts crucial to the determination that the Fisher Flouring Mills was a credit to the Northwest and the world:

The storage capacity for wheat at the mills was 2.5 million bushels, which represented 1,800 carloads, or approximately 30 solid train loads of wheat.

The leading product of the company was Fisher's Blend flour, a flour for "every purpose," but consumers also knew that Fisher had a wide variety of brands of flour in the warehouse awaiting shipment to all parts of the world.

A new Handysack Line was launched with items designed to meet certain needs. The products included ten different varieties of flours, cracked wheat, farina and cornmeal.

Fisher's cake flour had proven its superiority, and sales were increasing rapidly. Fisher's Biscuit Mix was specially prepared flour that needed only liquid added to be ready for use, thus shortening the time needed to create a baked item.

All of the "family" products of the Fisher Flouring Mills carried the Seal of Acceptance of the committee on foods of the American Medical Association. This was considered a distinct honor, meaning that the approval of this important organization had been given not only to the products but the advertising on the products. Consumers could be assured they were getting the best.

Consequently, the Fisher Flouring Mills was seen in a successful light, and Ziegler was justified in having the final words that Fisher was "America's finest flouring mills."

Longshore Strike of 1934 Had an Impact

While the Fisher Flouring Company was promoting flour with its star, Mary Mills, and handing out scones along with scone recipe cards at countless events, fairs, and demonstrations up and down the West Coast during the Great Depression years of the 1930s, a tempest was brewing off coastal ports. When the storm broke on the docks and warehouses, it resulted in a major strike, which had an economic ripple effect throughout the entire business world for the rest of the decade and beyond. Longshoremen struck on May 9, 1934, shutting docks down for two thousand miles of shoreline from Seattle and Tacoma to Portland, San Francisco, San Pedro and San Diego. The issues were wages and hours, and they wanted union representation. Most of all, they demanded elimination of a "shape-up" system whereby a hiring boss stood on the dock and picked workers for the day at random, or bias. They wanted a union hiring hall to replace that hated call-out procedure. The strike would last eighty-three days. Support was there. Truck drivers in San Francisco voted not to work on the docks. Teamsters in Seattle, Oakland and Los Angeles followed that lead. Sailors, firemen, cooks, stewards, masters, mates and pilots added their votes to strike. Suddenly, you had a "maritime" strike. Desperate employers urged the police to intervene and break the strike by force. Police broke up crowds of picketers in San Francisco, Seattle, Portland and elsewhere using clubs, tear gas and sawed-off shotguns. Newspapers reported 2 dead and 67 injured in San Francisco. But the battle wasn't over. Harry Bridges, an Australian immigrant, emerged as the strike leader, a militant bent on aiding the longshoremen cause. Longshoremen and supporters continued to clash with police, resulting in numerous arrests and beatings on both sides. When strikebreakers were permitted to work the port in Seattle, a mass of 600 Tacoma longshoremen led an invasion that grew to 2,000 men smashing down pier gates, driving police aside and halting all work. The violence continued with vigilantes ransacking union halls, destroying offices of a union newspaper and beating up strikers and supporters. The strike, despite all that brutality, was effective. Some 130,000 workers had left their jobs, an indication of widespread support. Laborer exceptions were made for those working in medical and hospital services, light and power, ferries and milk delivery. Still, the strike was losing steam. The longshoremen eventually gave in to arbitration. They were surprised but pleased to get their demands. Victory. The struggle set the stage for subsequent strikes in the following years on the docks with countless fights to achieve labor gains.

On another front, warehouse workers took advantage of the longshoremen-initiated strike to launch their own effort to organize for higher wages and greater job security. The effort had the support of the longshoremen. Warehouses and their workers were not confined to the docks. However, workers definitely were more active participants in maritime labor tasks at those facilities that were on the docks. Warehouse workers handled cargo brought off the ships by longshoremen. The Seattle warehouse union's initial action was an October 1935 strike against Fisher Flouring Mills. The Seattle Chamber of Commerce offered financial support for the mills and brought in strikebreakers to keep the mills open. However, the Seattle union gained overwhelming support from other labor unions that helped turn the tide. After a four-month fight, the strike, along with a boycott, produced a victory. In fact, the boycott of Fisher Mills' products had a remarkable effect: bakery workers as far away as the East Coast went on strike. Longshoremen and ship crews around the globe walked off ships rather than handle Fisher flour.

The labor disputes changed the way Fisher Flouring Company did business. From their beginning in 1911, the mills had mostly utilized ships to haul products from Seattle down the West Coast to warehouses on the docks of Tacoma, Portland, San Francisco, Los Angeles and San Diego. The decision was made to move the warehouses inland and move products by rail or truck, in what was deemed a cost-saving strategy.

FISHER FLOUR'S HOCKEY TEAM A BIG HIT

Fisher Flouring Mills Company determined in its infancy to build a market for its Blend flour, so it was important to reach people—namely, prospective customers—where people were as well as where they went. Thus, Fisher was more than willing to create a hockey team to play in what became Seattle's most prestigious amateur hockey league in the 1930s and 1940s, the City Hockey League. The league, founded in 1932, provided a high level of entertainment for fans for more than a decade, eventually giving way to the Pacific Coast Hockey League in 1944. Many times crowds of more than three thousand would flock to Civic Arena to view the games. Getting its name, Fisher's Blend Millers, in front of that many excited hockey fans was promotion at its best. How could folks not think of buying Fisher flour when they saw the team members wearing hockey sweaters with "Fisher's Blend" emblazoned on them? The Fisher team was competitive on the ice against the likes of Shurfine Groceries, Langendorf Bakery, Savidge Motors, Era's Grocery and Hullin Transfer. Fisher Flour's squad was at its best in 1938–39 when it was co-champion of the league with Shurfine Groceries.

In an era loaded with imaginative sports jargon in every sport, the City Hockey League was not ignored in that regard. An excerpt in the *Seattle Star* newspaper had this account of the season opener for Fisher Flours versus Savidge Motors in late October 1938, a goal-tending battle between Savidge veteran Romeo Charboneau and youngster Walt Batchelor, up from the junior hockey ranks, which Savidge won 1–0: "While Romeo stood in front of the iron pipes and batted out everything that came his way, brother Arm, that skookum defense veteran, provided the winner. Arm took a solo trip down the ice near the close of the second period and rapped the rubber biscuit home. But for that one poke which found the twine, Batchelor did a bang-up job in his first showing in front of the Fisher Flour nets for player/manager Bert Smith." In a November game, Batchelor "really earned his spurs," according to the *Seattle Star*, when against the Langendorf Thoro-breads, he held the bakery team scoreless while three Millers' defensemen, including Smith, were in the penalty box at the same time. Fisher won the game 3–1. It was the beginning of a streak that moved Bert Smith's crew up the standings and gave them confidence entering a matchup with league-leading Shurfine, which the Millers won handily 5–1. By the end of December, Fisher Flour scoring was evenly divided with veteran forwards Jack Close and Johnny Ferko leading the team with six goals and one assist and two goals and three

Left: Bert Smith was player/coach of the Fisher's Blend hockey team in Seattle's City League in the 1930s. *Photo by Roger Dudley from collection given to "Now and Then" authors Paul Dorpat and Jean Sherrard and then donated to the Seattle Public Library.*

Below: The Fisher's Blend float was a big hit at the 1939 Golden Jubilee parade in downtown Tacoma, celebrating Washington's fifty years of statehood. *Courtesy of Northwest Room, Tacoma Public Library.*

assists, respectively. Bert Smith had two goals and two assists. Fisher's Blend Millers eventually tied for the league championship when the City League season ended in February 1939.

The City Hockey League's 1939–40 season opened in October with Bert Smith gone, having moved to Corvallis, Oregon, for a new business opportunity. The team had many of the same players, but Arm Charboneau had assumed both of Smith's roles as manager and defenseman. Arm's brother, Romeo, still a goalie, had jumped to the Langendorf team. He obviously had an impact. Langendorf Bakery won the 1939–40 league championship.

PART IV

CONTINUING:
EMPHASIZE LINE, EXPAND

Zoom, MacArthur and a Country Band

Americans entered the 1940s with war clouds looming overhead, and it wasn't long before the conflict erupted. The Japanese bombed Pearl Harbor, an American naval base in the Hawaiian Islands, on December 7, 1941, and the United States declared war against Japan. Three days later, Nazi Germany declared war on the United States, and America found itself immersed in World War II against the Axis powers. Americans, having dealt with scarcities of commodities during the Great Depression, were suddenly facing more rationing of essentials such as sugar, milk, meat, coffee, eggs and breakfast cereals. Maybe the rationing situation for the good of the nation inspired Kenneth Robinson Fisher, grandson of family patriarch O.W. Fisher, to launch a cereal that required only hot water. Maybe he felt it was his duty after attempting to join the navy and being turned down because of vision issues and being told by a recruiter, "Ken, you should go back to the Fisher Flouring Mills and help with the war effort from there." Kenneth Fisher told that story in a wide-ranging interview conducted in the 1980s by the Museum of History and Industry (MOHAI) in Seattle. Fisher also related how he launched Zoom cereal to America and the world. That was something totally within his domain since he was the company's advertising manager and also was in charge of grocery products sales. "We released Zoom in the middle of a snowstorm, one of Seattle's worst in years, in January of 1943," Fisher said in the interview. For several days prior to the

Zoom, a breakfast cereal, was created and released in the 1940s by the Fisher Company and is still available today under the Krusteaz label. *The Erickson collection.*

launch, advertisements in Seattle newspapers had stated, "Zoom is coming! Zoom is coming." But on the day of Zoom's arrival, there were no newspaper stories, and transportation was at a standstill due to the inundation of snow. People were stuck at home listening to radio blurbs promoting Zoom cereal. Fisher said in the interview that NBC and its forty-five network stations nationally were blasting Zoom promotions, as were other local Seattle radio stations. Zoom was set to be distributed in twenty-six states.

Zoom was off the ground and running, so to speak, but people were slow to warm up to it, perhaps, reluctant to try something so radical. I mean, cereal without milk. Are you kidding? "We were in danger of losing Zoom distribution," Fisher said in the MOHAI interview. "We had to do something." Sometimes it's fortuitous how the tumblers fall into place and things work out. Well, that's what happened with Zoom cereal. Kenneth Fisher explained in the interview that Mills president O.D. Fisher (he assumed the position after O.W.'s death in 1922) "backed me on an imminent risk that had a chance to be successful." The company would offer a colored war map of the Pacific theater and Far East as a premium for purchasing Zoom cereal; send in a box top from Zoom along with 15 cents, and the company would send a map. "People really wanted the map," Fisher said. "The fact that we launched the promotion on the same day that General Douglas MacArthur returned to the Philippines on October 20, 1944, was an incredible coincidence. Zoom sold out in 26 states. The map was the key. But then, enough customers decided they liked Zoom and that turned our sales around." Zoom's success paved the way for sales of other Fisher products, Fisher noted.

Zoom cereal zoomed in popularity. It even sponsored a big-time radio show for a short run in 1946, featuring country music sensation Bob Wills and His Texas Playboys. The half-hour show was broadcast live on Tuesday nights from the Oakland (California) Auditorium Theatre on San Francisco's KGO Radio, an ABC network affiliate, and fed to sixteen other stations. Not sure how many stations picked up the show, except one did for sure, KMPC in Bakersfield, California. The master of ceremonies/announcer for the show was Jack Webb (yes, that star of later fame on TV's *Dragnet*). Webb would carefully follow the show script, but Wills often deviated, ad-libbed. A jingle to promote Zoom went like this:

> *For a breakfast that's delicious*
> *That will banish morning gloom*
> *Joe and Jane and Aloysius*
> *All eat instant-cooking Zoom.*

The jingle concluded with a trademark guitar lick by band member Junior Barnard. But listeners had the opportunity to send in four-line jingles as part of a contest. One night, this was a winning entry, performed by the band:

Me and Rosie felt so listless,
All the new folks passed us by
Zoom for breakfast made us peppy,
Now she's married…so am I.

It prompted Webb to announce: "Fishers…the millers of delicious Zoom… are sending five dollars to the writer of the Zoom jingle, who is Mrs. A. E. Oril, Box 1176, Marysville, Washington. Congratulations, Mrs. Oril." Then, he added, "Now let's zoom back to the fine entertainment of Bob Wills and the Texas Playboys." Later in the show, Webb appealed to listeners to request a special pamphlet that Fisher Flouring Mills was offering in cooperation with the U.S. government to help mitigate an international food emergency. "This pamphlet," he said, "will help you do your share in making supplies of wheat flour and cereals go farther. It will help you plan the 1,500-calorie menus that President Truman suggests we use two days a week. It also has tips on storing flour and cereals to prevent waste and spoilage. To get the free pamphlet, send your name and address to Bob Wills, Box 84, Seattle, Washington." As the show wound down, signaled by the band's closing rhythm theme, Webb barked a voice-over, "It's been Bob Wills and His Texas Playboys, brought to you by Fishers, millers of Zoom and other fine foods. Look for the name Fishers when you buy. This has been ABC, the American Broadcasting Company."

Zoom cereal remained a staple in Fisher's lineup in the 1950s and 1960s and well into the 1970s, when in 1977, Continental Mills took over Fisher's products. Zoom became a featured cereal on Continental's Krusteaz label. Continental has changed its name to the Krusteaz Company. And Zoom is still around today.

MEET ME AT THE FAIR

After closure for four years during World War II, the Western Washington Fair had a grand reopening in 1946 that launched a postwar renewal of all the things people loved about fairs—the animals, food, rides, entertainment, love of celebrating with others in a joyous crowd. It took them back to a happier time. Maybe they recalled stories told and retold about how the fair began in 1900. Perhaps, they ate Fisher scones and knew of their history. It all began in 1915 when Fisher scones came to the Valley Fair in Puyallup, Washington, and took the Northwest by surprise, folks flocking to get a taste of this special pastry item loaded with butter and raspberry jam. And raisins until the early 1970s. Interest has never waned, and people still flock to get their "fair" share of scones at this fair, which now is called the Washington State Fair, and at other county and regional fairs and events throughout the area. It's likely that, in the beginning, the Fisher Flouring Mills, which produced the scones, got butter for its biscuits from either Carnation or a dairymen's cooperative that eventually became Darigold. Those were the two prominent dairy operations in Washington State at that time. Jam came from William Hall (Paul) Paulhamus, one of the founders of the fair who produced Paul's Jams from his cannery operation in the Puyallup River Valley. Paulhamus had promised raspberry jam to the Fisher Company if it would bring its scones to the Valley Fair in the fall of 1915. He had invited the Fishers after he and his son, Dwight, tasted Fisher scones earlier that year at the Panama-Pacific Exposition in San Francisco. The fair, which began in 1900 as a three-day event to showcase animals and agriculture, grew steadily, and its name was changed to the Western Washington Fair in 1913, in response to increasing attendance from throughout the western part of the state. The fair's core values of education, family and fun have remained intact over the years, but attractions and activities have changed to stay relevant with the times. For instance, horse racing was an instant hit and continued to be popular with fairgoers until 1977, when the track was taken out. The grandstand was built and expanded over the years to accommodate the larger audiences the fair was attracting. Fisher scones were a big draw to the fair, other food concessions began in the 1920s and together they continue to fill people's appetites. Fisher scones have provided a constant thread as the fair has evolved with such highlighted changes as these: Earl Douglas brought the first carousel in 1923 on a horse-drawn wagon base, steam powered and featuring a Wurlitzer band organ, and today, this restored carousel is located in its own building in front of the Exposition Hall; during World War II, the federal government took over the fairgrounds and Japanese American citizens were interned there, causing the shutdown of the fair in 1942, 1943, 1944 and 1945 before a grand postwar reopening in 1946; in 1954, a new grandstand was

Made from raspberries grown in the Puyallup Valley, Paul's Jams was used for Fisher scones at their inaugural fair run in 1915. *The Erickson collection.*

This fair postcard could be sent to friends to let them know that all activities revolved around Fisher scones. *The Erickson collection.*

made of steel and concrete; the 1970 fair opened on schedule despite a fire that damaged the grandstand, part of the roller coaster, art and floral buildings and some concessions; the first Spring Fair was held in 1990 and continues today; major entertainment throughout the years included circuses in the early days, rodeos with world-class cowboys competing, and a long list of headliners such as Roy Rogers and Dale Evans, the Beach Boys, Kenny Rogers, Red Skelton, Tony Bennett, New Kids on the Block, Bob Hope, Ray Charles, Steppenwolf, Willie Nelson, Loretta Lynn, Kenny G., Frank Sinatra, the Oakridge Boys, Alabama, Hall & Oates, Chicago, Weird Al Yankovic, Bob Dylan, John Lee Hooker, Keith Urban, Macklemore, Heart, Blake Shelton, Carrie Underwood and the Doobie Brothers. The fair, renamed the Washington State Fair in 2013, goes on for most of September every year. And so do Fisher scones there.

There have been other fairs that have a longtime history, and here are some within Washington State where Fisher scones had or still have a presence:

THE KING COUNTY FAIR was founded in 1863, when Abraham Lincoln was president and Washington Territory was twenty-six years from statehood. The fair is believed to be the longest-running fair west of the Mississippi River. It began as a simple celebration of agriculture and originally took place in the Georgetown area of Seattle. The fair moved to Renton in 1900, and

Fisher scones draw customers because the tasty treats are considered "comfort food"— anytime, anywhere—including at this scone wagon in Enumclaw for the King County Fair. *Courtesy King County Fair.*

then to Enumclaw after World War II. It was part of Fisher Mills Company's repertoire and has continued to be a regular event on Conifer Specialties' schedule. Fisher scones have been a popular treat there for decades. The King County Fair is billed as "one of the last honest-to-goodness county fairs." It features country/western performers, animals, a rodeo, carnival rides, a variety of foods and all kinds of 4-H, FFA and grange displays. What better setting than surrounded by farms in the shadow of Mount Rainier? And there's still a lot of "country" dirt at the fairgrounds, as it hasn't been paved over as much as other fairs.

THE CENTRAL WASHINGTON STATE FAIR in Yakima, on the east side of the mountains, got its start in 1892 after the legislature resolved a brouhaha over which city—Yakima or Olympia—would be the state capital. The legislature chose Olympia but gave Yakima a consolation prize—the state fair. The fair was closed for one year during World War I, several years during the Great Depression of the 1930s due to financial issues, and then the Central Washington Fair Association was formed to restore stability. A four-year closure during World War II affected it and other fairs. It remains a draw for people interested in agricultural exhibits, carnival rides, popular entertainers and typical fair food. But Fisher scones, once a mainstay there, no longer have a presence.

THE SOUTHWEST WASHINGTON FAIR in Chehalis was originally served with Fisher scones by Fisher's Oregon distribution center, probably because of being closer to Portland than to Seattle. Once Conifer Specialties assumed responsibility in 1977 for what had been Fisher products, it took on the Southwest Washington Fair as one of the fairs it covered and continues that role today. The fair dates back to 1909, but the seeds for such an exhibition were planted in 1877 when a three-day event showcased agricultural products and animals of Lewis County. Continuous rain played havoc with the 1909 fair for its entire five-day run, but that didn't dampen spirits. The fair, in its early days, became well known for its racetrack, particularly featuring harness horse racing but also motorcycles and autos. One 1970s recollection in the book *Chapters of Life at the Southwest Washington Fair* quoted Nita Bonagofski, who noted, "As a Chehalis Rainbow Girl, I would ride on our float in the fair parade and sell scones at our fair booth. 'For only one thin dime,' I would say as the 'barker.' National Fruit donated the raspberry jam, Darigold the butter, and Sandy's Bakery in Chehalis donated the use of its facility to make the scones." The fair has always been a showcase for

4-H and FFA products and animals and has evolved to feature carnival rides, entertainers, destruction derbies, food and even Bengal tigers. The Southwest Washington Fair keeps going and growing with a philosophy driven by the premise that the fair "is always new to somebody."

THE EVERGREEN STATE FAIR in Monroe became such when the Snohomish County Fair renamed itself in 1949. The county's fair roots go back to an impromptu fair in 1874, in which the winning agricultural products were forwarded to competition at the Territorial Fair in Olympia. Subsequently, there were other fairs that cropped up in Snohomish County over the decades that followed, including ones in the cities of Everett and Snohomish, competing for fairgoers. Then fairs shut down and found a home in Granite Falls for a while; they later popped up with a variety of fairs around Monroe, becoming the Cavalcade of the Valleys into the 1930s and early 1940s. Finally, following the Second World War, the Snohomish

Left: Compared to the slick computerized cash registers of today, this rusty old register discovered in a storeroom at the Evergreen State Fair in Monroe seems like a real dinosaur, but it's a reminder of yesteryear at that longtime fair. *Courtesy A.J. Milliken collection.*

Right: After the pandemic shut down the 2020 fair, the Evergreen State Fair returned in 2021 with COVID-19 protocols in place and a souvenir shirt that exclaimed, "Back in the Saddle Again!" *Photo by author.*

County Fair was first held in Monroe in 1946 and then rebranded the Evergreen State Fair three years later. All the usual fair attractions are there, from agricultural displays, animal judging, horse shows and carnivals to entertainers and food offerings. Fisher scones have been a constant. The Evergreen Speedway, the only NASCAR venue in Washington, has stock car racing as part of the fair schedule.

Then there are events and fairs where Conifer no longer has a presence, but other groups sell Fisher scones, sometimes using the Fisher Fair Scone & Short Cake Mix. That's been the case with Dry Creek Grange, which has purchased Fisher Fair Scone & Short Cake Mix from Conifer Specialties and made scones at the Clallam County Fair on Washington's Olympic Peninsula for more than three decades. Conifer has sold Fisher Fair Scone & Short Cake Mix to volunteer groups raising funds for use in their communities. For the four-day Clallam County Fair in August 2022, it proved a big challenge to reboot the event, after the COVID-19 pandemic forced the fair's closure in 2020 and 2021, said Cindy Kelly, who has volunteered in the grange's scone booth for thirty-two years and heads the group's scone-making operation. "We got the scone mix from Conifer, and we were glad to get it," she said. "We don't call our scones 'Fisher,' we call them 'Dry Creek.'" Kelly said they had a bit of a problem with the jam, noting that Trailblazer, the brand the grange had always used, no longer had raspberry jam in five-gallon buckets, only thirty-two-ounce glass jars. That wouldn't work. They needed buckets of jam. After some taste-testing, grange members decided to go with a four-berry Trailblazer mix—raspberry, blackberry, strawberry and blueberry. Kelly said they received no complaints at this year's fair.

PHELPS FISHER HAD A FULFILLING LIFE

Born in 1934, Phelps Fisher was not even a teenager when he got his introduction into the Fisher family business. "I was twelve years old and *the* work ethic was firmly established in my family," he recounted in an interview in May 2022, adding, "It was clear that I needed to spend my summers working so I started my career at the Fisher Flouring Mills on Harbor Island." Fisher said his first job was to serve as a messenger during a period of construction that temporarily removed the pneumatic tubes that allowed information to process from the order desk out to the mill.

"Basically, I became the replacement," he mused, "sitting in a chair in one of the offices and they'd call me and yell, 'Fisher, go to the order desk.'" He said he'd run, literally, to get the information and continue running to take it to wherever it needed to go in a very large facility. Then he returned to the office where he had been stationed and waited for the next assignment. "It was a very busy milling operation with ships coming and going all day long and I did that for a full summer when I was twelve," he noted. "I never had a summer off the rest of my life until I retired fully." And that was nearly seven decades later. One of the perks of that first summer, he said, was that, as part of payment for his work, he received one share of stock in the company. So, at thirteen, Phelps Fisher was able to attend shareholder meetings as probably the youngest shareholder. Pretty heady stuff, he thought. At about that same age, he said, "I ate my first Fisher scone at the Puyallup Fair," which he attended with his parents, Kenneth and Margarett Fisher. "The scone was so tasty. I loved it." In late December 1946, the family took a trip, driving to California. He recollected, "We're having a good time in Palm Springs and my grandmother in Seattle had a heart attack and my mother and little sister had to fly back home, and

Phelps Fisher's favorite personal photo of the historic Fisher Flouring Mills. *Courtesy of Phelps Fisher.*

it rained for three days in Palm Springs. So, my father said we're going to Los Angeles where we spent a week attending one to three radio shows a day. Because he was the advertising manager for Fisher Flouring Mills, he was able to get instant access to whatever shows he wanted." Phelps Fisher said it was his first exposure to live radio shows sponsored by advertisers. "Radio was really big, and I got a good sense of how that market worked and what the broadcasts were all about," he said.

Fisher's summer employment continued through his junior year of college in a variety of mill jobs, ranging from sweeping floors to packing flour in bags. One summer, he visited a buddy in Minneapolis and was able to get a job unloading rail cars at Pillsbury Flour Mills. Fisher said he worked hard to earn fifteen credits with satisfactory grades per quarter at the University of Washington or else risk being eligible for the draft for military service. He was also "running second" in his air force ROTC class and had to make a commitment by the end of his sophomore year. But the air force determined it wasn't going to accept anyone but those able to become a pilot, and that left Fisher out because of a vision issue. He continued taking courses. By the end of his junior year, he had finished all of the requirements for a bachelor's degree in business administration. He took a full-time job as a floor director at KOMO-TV and was allowed to take broadcast courses during his senior year, with the army indicating he could get a direct commission as a television production specialist after college graduation. When that time came, however, Fisher was told the army no longer needed TV production specialists. So, Fisher was eligible for the draft and reported as required. He was sent to a doctor because of a sinus condition, the result of an allergy he had contracted to flour dust during his summer jobs at the Fisher Mills, an unforeseen development that ended any milling aspirations he might have had. The doctor asked Fisher if such a condition would prohibit military service, and Fisher replied, "No, sir." So, he assumed he'd get a draft notice but instead got a letter determining he was unacceptable for military service. He said he often thought that being honest about his situation contributed to a decision made on his behalf. So, Fisher continued his job as a floor director. As such, he worked alongside a camera in the studio, and tasks included helping plan the programming, supervising equipment setup, giving cues and time counts to presenters and actors and rehearsing live shows or commercial shootings.

KOMO-TV and Radio were part of the Fisher family empire, and the stations were devoted to promoting Fisher's Blend flour, so some commercials were made to accent that. Fisher Flour also sponsored programming, particularly on radio. "Fisher was an advertiser, but not a significant advertiser on the local market," Phelps Fisher recalled. "My father [Kenneth] was the advertising manager for Fisher Mills and in the 1940s and 1950s, he bought primarily radio advertising. In the thirteen western states you could buy network radio advertising on a regional basis, and that's what he did so well." He said celebrities would come to the television station and film commercials promoting Fisher Flour and, ultimately, Fisher scones. "One of the people I met was Betty White, whom I remember specifically filming commercials at KOMO-TV for Fisher Flour and other products," Fisher said. "I had to go [to] the airport to pick up Allen Ludden (White's husband) for a client party." Ludden was a TV actor, singer, emcee and game show host.

Like his father, Phelps Fisher also had a keen business sense and a knack for doing the right thing, and he rose up the ladder of success. He stayed in broadcast business sales, moved to sales and marketing and set up a marketing department across multiple stations. Fisher had stations in Seattle and Portland (Oregon) and eventually had stations throughout the Pacific Northwest and California. As marketing director, Phelps Fisher said, he recalled having to go to Portland to set up a cooperative marketing plan with Seattle/Portland stations to attract regional advertisers. He was a busy man who landed on controlling boards, too. "I ended up on the boards of KOMO-TV and Radio, and KATU-TV in Portland," Fisher said. "I ended up on the boards of Fisher Mills and other Fisher properties and enterprises. I wound up on the board of everything the company had as a fairly young person, all the while, working as an employee." He said it was an interesting role for him. "I'm on the boards and also not a senior officer in any of the companies," Fisher said, "and working to maintain good relationships and the respect of other board members without creating conflict or being seen as a problem. That's a good responsibility for a young person and it allowed me to learn a tremendous amount." He followed his father's advice for success, which was in line with the whole Fisher family philosophy: work hard and be honest. They might also add: Get to know and be involved in the community in which you live. And try to avoid calling attention to yourself. "How do you avoid attention when you're making a big impact like the Fisher family was? Well, you cannot avoid it but there's a difference

Phelps Fisher's cap marking the seventy-fifth anniversary of the Fisher Flouring Mills. *Courtesy of Phelps Fisher.*

between seeking exposure versus quietly going about your business and not calling attention to yourself," Fisher told me.

The Fisher Company was supportive of the community and encouraged its employees to get involved. Phelps Fisher said, "I wouldn't have been able to do all the things I did without the support of Christel, my wife of sixty-two years." He recalled that he was allowed time during the workday to attend meetings of many boards, with the first being the Boys Clubs of Seattle and King County when he was young. "I was the youngest person sitting in those meetings but the company knew this was an opportunity for me to meet potential clients and get the pleasure of serving the community, which was important to me and the company," Fisher said. As Fisher became executive vice-president/marketing for the corporation and later chairman of the board, he wielded influence and served on boards of such community groups as the Fred Hutchinson Cancer Research Institute, the Downtown Seattle Association, the Northwest Kidney Center, the Better Business Bureau of the Northwest and the Puget Sound Blood Center, which evolved to become Bloodworks Northwest. He was particularly proud of serving on a committee that helped move that organization to regional status and change its name. Another proud moment, he said, was when he was part of an effort to allow girls in the boys' clubs, despite the charter prohibiting it. "We told New York authorities at the Boys Club we were going to do it," Fisher recalled, "and if they didn't approve it and change their charter to include girls, we were going to affiliate with someone else." The outcome? "They approved it and made it the Boys and Girls Clubs," he said, smiling.

The Fisher Company worked hard to market its Blend flour, Fisher scones and other biscuit and bread mixes, as well as cereals such as Zoom, which Fisher invented and which is still available, as are its other products since the company relinquished that business to Continental Mills in the late 1970s. How and why did that come about? The flour and food products business had become highly competitive, Phelps Fisher said, "and you really had to make a decision about whether to go national to get the economics you needed in order to have a product be successful. What's it going to take and what's the financial pressure to compete with national brands?" Thus, he said, the decision was made to "move the product to somebody who was in that category," and that happened to be Continental Mills. A separate company, Fisher Scones Inc., was formed to sell Fisher scones and evolved to become Conifer Specialties. Conifer serves Fisher scones, made from the same recipe developed by Fisher Mills more than a century ago, at many dozens of fairs and expos in Washington State, using permanent booths and

Phelps Fisher, great-grandson of O.W. Fisher, holds an Emmy Award he won and a bag of Fisher scones he received as a gift. *Photo by Keith Erickson.*

trailers, as well as at numerous shopping centers, farms and grocery stores with its food truck. After the change, Fisher Mills continued to produce bulgur for Asian markets until the mills was sold to Pendleton Flour Mills in 2001 and Fisher got out of the flour business, turning its resources to the broadcast side of its business.

KOMO-TV, which was an ABC network station, had a skilled news staff that won countless awards over many years, and sometimes when Fisher tired of meetings in his chairman's office with lawyers, consultants and financial advisers, he'd go down and spend an hour in the newsroom. Having felt he had a role in shaping their success, he said, he'd bask in the "excitement of what was going on there and I would tell the staff, 'This is what we do and why we're here, right?' and also add, 'You guys are great and I just feel better when I get a chance to come down here and be with you.'"

Phelps Fisher worked diligently to support the KOMO-TV news staff, and, as mentioned before, loved to associate with them, and they valued his involvement. When Jim Clayton ended his forty-year broadcast career with his final six years as vice-president and general manager at

KOMO-TV, he sent Phelps Fisher an e-mail on his last day in 2012 that stated: "I wanted to thank you for your support over the past six years. You assembled a remarkable group of people who made me proud every day. I always appreciated your interest and valued your input. It's been an honor and a privilege to know you and to guide the KOMO staff." KOMO-TV made sure Phelps Fisher got an Emmy in 2013 when KOMO-TV won an impressive fifteen Northwest regional Emmys, including the prestigious Station Excellence Award. After interviewing Fisher at his Bellevue home, I asked my son Keith, who had accompanied me, to take a photo of Fisher with the Emmy and the bag of Fisher scones we had brought him.

I called Phelps Fisher a few days later and inquired how he liked the scones. He said he enjoyed them and shared some with family members. "I zapped a scone for twenty seconds in the microwave," he explained, "then put it on a plate, sat down at the kitchen table, and took fifteen minutes eating the scone in little slices with a fork." In other words, he savored it. He said he remembered his first scone in the late 1940s while attending the Puyallup Fair with his parents. How did the scones we brought compare to the ones of his childhood? "Just as tasty," he said, pausing. He added a comment that confirmed the proverbial impression of customers: "Scones were larger years ago, I'd say about 20 percent bigger." So, there you have the definitive word. He had some other thoughts. "I love scones and many people do," Fisher mused. "I think it's because scones are unique compared to everything else. They're not something you can get everywhere. Scones are thoughtful treats, special treats." He offered a final reflection on the irony of what has transpired with the Fisher Flour Mills gone but Fisher scones still around. "Today, no one remembers the Fisher Flouring Mills, but they sure remember Fisher scones," he asserted. "And we're remembered because of the name."

FISHER DEDICATED TO ALL ITS PRODUCTS, FROM SCONES TO BULGUR

After the Fisher Flouring Mills divested itself of its product line, including Fisher Flour and Fisher scones, in the late 1970s, it continued to focus on the production of bulgur to ship to other countries until the year 2000, when the mills was sold to Pendleton Mills, an Oregon plant that shut down the Fisher facility a year later. Fisher had been providing ala, a modern American version of the ancient bulgur, since 1958. When the company launched the product to the marketplace following a three-year development process, the mills president and general manager John L. Locke was optimistic, firmly stating that he believed that bulgur would hold its own in nutritional benefits as a rice substitute for Far East consumers. More than three million pounds of ala were shipped in the first commercial cargo aboard the American Mail Line's *Java Mail* bound for Korea as a consignment to the Korean Society for the Promotion of Bulgur Wheat. Fisher's involvement began shortly after U.S. president Dwight D. Eisenhower on July 10, 1954, signed into law the legislation that would become known as the Food for Peace Act. The Food for Peace program is the largest U.S. food assistance endeavor and, in conjunction with its partners, has helped, to date, over nearly seventy years, some 4 billion people in 150 countries. Immediately after President Eisenhower's action, the Fisher Company decided to participate in the program and began to develop a process designed to retain all of the nutritive value of the original wheat kernel. The result was a small cracked kernel about two-thirds the size of a rice kernel with a water content reduced to 10 percent made from surplus Pacific Northwest white wheat. Considerable promotion was done prior to the huge commercial release in June 1958. Actively involved in that effort were the Washington Wheat Growers Association, the Oregon Wheat Growers League and the U.S. Department of Agriculture. Small batches of ala were even shipped during this period as tests to gauge feedback. Then, Fisher Mills launched its massive program to provide bulgur, a valuable food staple to people living in other parts of the world, including Asia and South America. The guiding philosophy was the same as when it provided Fisher scones for the masses—bring bulgur to as many people where they live as possible.

As a journalist always wanting to answer questions I believe readers might have, I sought to find the meaning behind the word *ala* in reference to bulgur. The owners of Sunnyland Mills, of Fresno, California, billed as the largest commercial producer of bulgur in the United States, didn't know why bulgur was called "ala." I had to go to Turkey, bulgur's country of origin, to find the answer. The expert was Dr. Mustafa Bayram, a dean and professor in the Department of Food Engineering at the University of Gaziantep. He has taught classes and written countless articles on food issues, particularly the quality and characteristics of wheat bulgur. Dr.

Bayram told me the name *ala* is similar to the grain's name in Turkish but is of Arabic origin, and it has three definitions: (1) A combination of several colors (mixed), (2) A color between brown and red and (3) "Special good, very good." He told me that "ala" on the label of a flour bag, such as that of the Fisher Flouring Company, was, in his opinion, "an indication

Opposite: Bags of bulgur wheat (ala) being loaded on a ship bound for Korea in the late 1950s. *The Erickson collection.*

Left: These bags were filled with bulgur wheat and shipped to countries around the globe. *The Erickson collection.*

Below: The Fisher Flouring Mills still going strong, shown in this photo (est. 1960). *The Erickson collection.*

of numbers 2 and 3." By being among the first to develop bulgur for consumption in the world, the Fisher Company showed the innovativeness prevalent throughout its history and a testament to the longtime production of its Northwest favorite, Fisher scones.

A Family That Makes Scones Together
Stays Together

Frances Ryland, a ninety-five-year-old Portland (OR) woman, has fond memories of working, along with her late husband, Raymond, at Fisher Flouring Mills' distribution center in Portland from the 1950s well into the 1980s, and her son Dwayne talked about selling Fisher scones with his brother, Dennis, and sister, Diana, when they were teenagers. "Fisher had three divisions—grocery, bakery and feed—and Ray and I were in grocery when we started in 1952," Frances Ryland recounted. She noted that Ray worked until 1976, when his job was terminated. Continental Mills took over Fisher's business in 1977. Frances said she had become full time in 1970 and continued to sell Fisher products for Continental until her job went away in 1986. "Over the years, we sold different types of flour, mixes, breakfast cereals Zoom and farina and bulgur ala wheat," she said. Dwayne interjected that he and his siblings sold scones at different fairs or festivals and loved the experience. "It was the best summer jobs we could ever have," he maintained.

Raymond Ryland was the man behind a major shift in the Fisher Company's strategy. He had an idea, his family reported, and he presented it to the top Fisher echelon: build a scone wagon, a trailer with an oven that you can transport to locations to make and sell scones. Previously, the company had rented space in permanent buildings at fairs—such as the Oregon State Fair in Salem, where Ryland managed Fisher scones sales, starting in 1964—and hauled supplies to sell scones. The Fisher hierarchy liked the idea, and a forty-foot-long, fully equipped trailer with generator and oven was built. Fisher's first-of-its-kind trailer debuted at the Pat Boone Golf Tournament in Ocean Shores, Washington, in the 1960s and, subsequently, became a regular feature at Oregon events, including the Portland Rose Festival, Multnomah County Fair and Lane County Fair. And more trailers were to come. Frances often joined Raymond selling scones, as did their

The giant Scotch Tam (hat) on the roof of the Fisher Scone building at Pixieland in the early 1970s was a full 32 feet in diameter. More than 1,200 square feet of fiberglass mat, more than sixty gallons of resin and more than 400 feet of steel bar were used in the construction. For a scone, the price was fifteen cents, and for a shortcake, thirty-five cents. *The Erickson collection.*

children. Fisher's Oregon operation also was responsible for selling scones at the Southwest Washington Fair in Chehalis and at a specially constructed building that resembled a Scottish hat with a tam on top at Pixieland, an amusement park that existed for a few years in the 1970s near Lincoln City on the Oregon coast. Occasionally, the scone wagon would venture out to some impromptu location, such as the time it dropped in at a grocery store in Astoria on the coast, and KATU-TV, a Fisher-owned Portland station, covered the trailer's presence there.

"I enjoyed making scones a lot," said Frances Ryland, "but it was hard work, usually from eight in the morning to ten at night." She noted that scones were being sold for fifteen cents apiece or seven for a dollar, and when the price got raised to twenty cents, some people complained. "I told them a hamburger cost way more than that," she quipped. Sales were brisk, maybe close to $4,000 a day at events such as the Rose Festival, but not so good at Pixieland, for instance, where sales were seen more as a means to simply promote Fisher's flour. Pixieland never made it as an amusement park ("who would want to go there in the winter when it's pouring down rain?" some critics opined). The site has been returned to nature. Dwayne often helped his mother answer interview questions. For example, he explained that there was a scone mix that only required water when his parents began their Fisher careers. The Fisher's Blend flour was still available, however, and people could make scones using that but would have had to add milk, shortening and other dry ingredients. But the scone recipe was no longer advertised in newspapers as it had been in the 1930s and 1940s for marketing purposes. The couple worked out of Fisher offices located on Washington Street in Portland. After Fisher, Raymond Ryland found other work in the food services industry. Frances was eventually transferred to another location in north Portland and ended her career there.

PART V

TRANSFORMING: FISHER TO CONTINENTAL

ROSE CHARTERS CREATED KRUSTEAZ PIE CRUST MIX

Interestingly, Continental Mills, which eventually took over the selling and distribution of Fisher Mills products in the late 1970s, got its start in the kitchen of an innovative Seattle woman in the 1930s at the same time a woman with the promotional name of Mary Mills was pitching Fisher's Blend flour and Fisher scones. Sometimes, things come together to create the perfect situation for change to occur. That was the case for Rose Charters. The Great Depression made things difficult. Money was tight, jobs were scarce, and families needed ingredients such as butter, milk, eggs and cooking oil to add to flour or even premade baking mixes in order to make items for meals. So, when a resourceful woman in her midfifties, working in her kitchen, happened to create a pie crust mix that needed just water, that was an incredible occurrence. An opportunity. Rose Charters was thinking not only of saving money in her household but also maybe even making money on the side, if she could sell the pie mix. She started selling the pie crust mix, which she called "crust ease" (get it?), to friends, neighbors and local cafés. Of course, the name morphed to Krusteaz, which has become known worldwide. Anyway, demand outstripped supply. Rose and her husband, James, who had incorporated their company as Continental Mills in October 1932, suddenly had to find a location that could serve as a small manufacturing plant. With a loan from investors in his hometown of Chicago, James was able to open a shop with a handful of employees. The rest, as they say, was history for

Rose and James as their pie crust mix became popular. Who would have thought that a woman from a Washington State pioneering family would invent such an innovative food product? But, then again, maybe it should not be that surprising when you imagine that someone who was the ninth of thirteen children, whose father was Samuel Love Gilbreath, the first white settler of then Washington Territory's Columbia County. When you have that many siblings, you probably have to be pretty creative. Born in 1876 on a farm near Dayton, Ada Rose Gilbreath attended Washington Agricultural College (later Washington State University), started teaching in Walla Walla, moved to Seattle to continue that career and married her husband in 1918.

The Washington Agricultural College, in the 1890s when Rose Gilbreath was a student, was recognized as one of the leading research institutions in the country, and I'm guessing she came away with knowledge that paid dividends when she was trying to develop a baking mix product in her kitchen years later during the Great Depression. By 1941, Continental Mills had sold "in excess" of one million packages of the Krusteaz pie crust mix over its first eight years, which was an average of 125,000 packages per year, according to a *Seattle Times* story. Four years later, John J. Heily was asked to sit on the board of Continental Mills. The request came from Heily's brother-in-law Tom O'Bryan, one of the original Chicago investors. O'Bryan reportedly wanted someone to watch over his investment. Heily, with his background in sales, eventually joined the company and was able to help Continental navigate through some tougher times with World War II raging. Early in his tenure, Heily hired a food chemist who helped expand the company's product line to include cake, doughnut and biscuit mixes. Heily's reward was being named president of Continental Mills in 1947. The next development a year or so later was the introduction of a Krusteaz just-add-water buttermilk pancake mix, created in partnership with the University of Washington's Home Economics Department. The Charters were still involved and listed as vice-presidents in the company.

Sometime after 1964, when James Charters died and Continental Mills was flourishing, Rose Charters sold her shares in the company to the Heily family. The Charters had no children, so it seemed like the thing to do. Rose Charters died in 1970. A few years later, John J. Heily, who had previously made his son, John M. Heily, vice-president, relinquished his titles of president and CEO to his son. In 1975, John M. Heily secured a major contract to supply kitchens for the Trans-Alaska Pipeline System. While Continental had to scramble to develop new recipes and revamp its operation, the result was big profits for this new vital enterprise. A couple of years later, Continental took over the product line of Fisher Flouring Mills and formulated a company, Conifer Specialties, to handle some of that distribution but mainly provide a continuation of Fisher scones featured at the many fairs and other locations in Washington State and elsewhere. John M. Heily's sons, Andy and Pat, have been involved in the business over the years. Andy took over as president and CEO of Continental in 2015. Pat has primarily been involved with Conifer. John M. Heily died in September 2019 while the Washington State Fair was in full swing. Andy and Pat are carrying on the family tradition. While Continental no longer packs Fisher's Blend flour, it does provide Fisher Fair Scone & Short Cake Mix for Conifer's business operation at fairs and food truck venues. In late 2022, Andy Heily announced that Continental had changed its name to the Krusteaz Company. It somehow seemed appropriate considering its beginnings in a Seattle woman's kitchen many decades ago and the popularity of Krusteaz mixes still today.

Mike Maher's Love for Scones Never Waned

For Mike Maher, CEO of Conifer Specialties, which sells the famous Fisher scones at dozens of fairs, festivals and events throughout Washington State, it was love at first bite. Maher tasted his first scone as a high school student in the late 1970s while working at a scone booth at the Rose Festival in Portland, Oregon. He was hooked. He still is today. Maher got his start shortly after Conifer took over scone sales from the Fisher Flouring Mills, which had been marketing the scrumptious product since 1911. Conifer officials invited Maher back the following year. Later, after graduation from the University of Oregon with a degree in business management, he went to work full time for the company. He's been its strongest advocate for scones ever since. Scones have evolved over time: butter, raspberry jam and raisins in the early days; raisins eventually taken out, replaced by specially mixed honey butter and raspberry jam; finally butter and raspberry jam. The constant has been the jam, although suppliers have changed during the passing of more than a century. Prices have changed, as well. Fisher Flouring Mills either gave them away free or charged a nickel apiece because its objective was to promote its flour. Today (2022), a scone is its own valued commodity and sells for three dollars apiece, with the bargain being a baker's dozen (thirteen) for twenty-eight dollars or a half dozen for fifteen dollars. What hasn't changed, however, is people's unrelenting appetite. "Everywhere I go, I run into people who love scones," Maher said. Scones are the backbone of Conifer's business, with sales of more than 1.5 million alone at what is billed as the Washington State Fair in Puyallup, Washington, over twenty-one days in September. They sell hundreds of thousands more collectively at other fairs and events throughout the year.

But Conifer is a diversified entity that also owns Canterbury Cuisine, Canterbury Naturals and Canterbury Organics and manufactures and sells more than two hundred Canterbury packaged mixes, ranging from soups and desserts to drinks. It has even branched into the gift world, supplying mixes to catalogue and school fundraising companies. But even if Conifer continues to expand to keep pace with a

Mike Maher, president and CEO of Conifer Specialties, a huge lover of Fisher scones, is enthusiastic about spreading that love to others. *Photo by author.*

competitive market, Maher said, the company will always rely on its inroads in the community to sell Fisher scones. That will never go away because people won't let it. And Conifer knows that the treat is its bread, or, scone and butter (jam added). When the coronavirus caused fairs and other big-crowd events to be canceled in 2020 and restricted somewhat in 2021, Conifer was fortunate to have a food truck that had been operating for several years. The truck kept going, taking scones to many locations—supermarkets, farms, pumpkin patches and other venues. It paid off, bringing in revenue that was lost from closed fairs, festivals and events. More importantly, Maher said, "It kept the company's main product in front of the public. After all, it's a big part of our identity. We get so much recognition from Fisher scones." For Maher, scones are a part of his life and always will be. He treasures the tradition and history behind the Northwest delicacy. He collects Fisher memorabilia. One of his favorite parts of the job is dropping in on Fisher booths and sampling the wares. He also has been known to jump right in and help—flattening dough balls, cutting them into four triangular-shaped biscuits, putting them on trays. Then, when the freshly baked hot scones are dumped on the hot table, he gets busy buttering or jamming or bagging scones. All with a smile, because he loves the excitement of serving customers waiting patiently to order. "I understand why people wait in line for a half hour or more to get scones," Maher said. "They love scones, they have memories of scones as

Conifer's food truck is a welcome sight for customers because it comes to shopping centers and other venues close to them. *Photo by Keith Erickson.*

kids and now they're here with their kids. I get that. When I talk to people, I watch their eyes light up and hear their stories tumble forth. It's part of Northwest history. And I'm very proud of that history."

Maher has generated a lot of that history himself, as a result of his many years working and guiding the Fisher scone–making company to thousands of events and fairs for close to half a century. He remembers working a circuit with a crew and going many places. "We didn't check in," he related, "we moved from town to town. We had a one-ton truck with supplies and pulled a mobile scone wagon. One time they wanted me to drive, and I was really nervous. With those big semis on the road, I felt like I was getting sucked in." Since the beginning of Conifer's management of the Fisher Scones operation, Conifer has gone to most of the fairs for many years in the nineteen counties in western Washington, including the Northwest Fair in Lynden, the Evergreen State Fair in Monroe and, of course, the Western Washington Fair (rebranded the Washington State Fair) in Puyallup, and the Spring Fair in Puyallup. Fisher scones also were sold at the Ellensburg Rodeo in eastern Washington. Fisher scones were also a favorite at the Oregon State Fair in Salem and the Pacific National Exhibition (PNE) in Vancouver, British Columbia. Many were the same ones that the Fisher Company had gone to, but over time, some went away. Maher explained it became a situation where some were out of reach, and it was a timing issue being able to take down at one fair and get to another to set up. For instance, Conifer no longer goes to the Oregon State Fair, the PNE, the Ellensburg Rodeo, the Northwest Fair and a number of county fairs. "It's been a give and take," Maher mused. "We've pulled some fairs, added some events. I think we're doing more than we did historically." Some of the events that have been added to the Fisher Scone schedule have included: the Taste of Tacoma, the Bite of Seattle, the Bellevue Arts Museum Arts Fair and the Veterans Day Parade in Auburn. Others have been held on the Puyallup fairgrounds, where Conifer has its scone trailers and supplies stored and where several other permanent buildings are available for making and selling scones. Events there have included the Good Guys Car Show, A Victorian Country Christmas and the Washington Sportsmen Show. Plus, Conifer built another food truck so it now has two that go to locations around western Washington, such as grocery store parking lots, farmers' markets and neighborhood festivals. "We want to keep bringing Fisher scones to people," Maher said. "I don't think we've hit our capacity there yet." While Conifer is always looking for new innovations, such as scone ice cream (vanilla with scone chunks and raspberry jam) recently available in stores, Maher said it's hard to know how to improve scones themselves. "Scones are best right out of the oven," Maher insisted. "And you really don't want to mess around with what's inside. People like them the way they are—namely, with butter and raspberry jam."

PART VI

LIVING:
PEOPLE SHARE SCONE FEELINGS

UNDER THE GRANDSTAND
WAS WHERE LEONA ELDER WAS

If there were a song fitting for longtime Fisher Scone worker/manager Leona Elder, the lyrics would have to be: "Under the grandstand we'll be making fresh scones, under the grandstand people waiting in line, under the grandstand we'll be feelin' so fine, under the grandstand, grandstand." This to the tune of the Drifters' hit song "Under the Boardwalk." Leona Elder has worked exclusively for more than three and a half decades at the Fisher Scone booth under the grandstand on the fairgrounds in Puyallup at what is now called the Washington State Fair, which runs during Septembers. "I still call it the 'Puyallup Fair' and that's what it will always be to me," said Elder, who vowed to keep going until she puts in forty years. She was a single mother raising three children when she was hired by Conifer Specialties and began working nights at the fair to help make ends meet. By her fourth year, she was managing the scone team, a testament to her office and administrative skills honed in her full-time behavioral health job with Group Health. She's retired from Kaiser Permanente, which acquired Group Health in 2017. But not from scones just yet. Over the years, Elder worked alongside her crew in various tasks. Often, she was upstairs in a room overlooking the grandstand booth doing the paperwork so essential to making sure the operation ran smoothly: keeping track of revenue from sales and hours worked by the many part-time employees, determining supplies that needed to be replenished, hiring and firing if needed. "I never worked anywhere else (but under the grandstand) and I loved the fact that all we sold were scones," said Elder, who eventually switched to days. She noted that, unlike other scone locations on the fairgrounds, the booth under the grandstand didn't sell strawberry shortcakes or beverages. Just scones. And only scones. Fairgoers loved scones and especially under the grandstand, which was first location that ever sold the tasty morsels and the only one for many years. It seemed like it was tradition to get scones there on the Puyallup fairgrounds. The original booth was so steeped in tradition, folks were drawn to it and important things happened there.

Elder recalled that a television crew came one time to film the scone crew for a national food channel, showing all aspects of the making of Fisher scones, from dough to buttered-and-jammed scones and the tasty morsels bagged in glassine. She said the TV crew was particularly intrigued by the dough ball–making machine that dated back to the 1930s or 1940s. Politicians, she said, loved to show up at the booth under the grandstand because it generated quite a crowd, and you know what a crowd means? Potential voters. Elder remembered Christine Gregoire and Gary Locke, both Washington governors, trying their hands on the hot table, buttering, jamming and bagging scones. Denny Heck also made an appearance in the booth when he was a Washington State congressman. Elder has also experienced the noise of the numerous concerts over the years and folks above the scone booth in grandstand seats shaking the whole place. But there was only one time Elder worried that the structure above her and her crew would collapse on them, and that was during the 1989 concert by New Kids on the Block in the midst of their popularity. "The place was jammed with eight- to thirteen-year-old fans and things were shaking," she recounted. "I thought [the grandstand] would come apart." Of course, the scone booth was busy after that concert, as it is after most acts, because people want their scones. Even "neighboring" vendors under the grandstand appreciated the scone booth. Elder recalls that one nearby booth that sold pianos "always played Happy Birthday" to any celebrating scone worker.

Leona Elder was blessed to have a crew that included family members—children and grandchildren—to make for a meaningful experience and fond memories. Maybe less stressful, too. "You can see, I don't have any gray hair," she quipped. "My kids have more gray hair than I do." One time, Elder said, Conifer CEO Mike Maher, seeing all of her family, kidded her about the family connection, saying, "If you quit, there goes half the staff." Elder

Leona Elder, longtime manager of the scone location under the grandstand at the fair in Puyallup, has made many memories over her thirty-five-year run. *Photo by author.*

Scone manager Leona Elder poses with then U.S. congressman Denny Heck (*center*) and Pat Heily. Heck had stopped by to work on the hot table, and Heily, a member of the Heily family that owns Conifer Specialties, lent his support. *Courtesy of Conifer Specialties.*

has loved being part of the Conifer family and relished a great relationship with Maher, noting, "Mike is one of the kindest persons I've ever met." She's also loved being at "the best fair, one of the top ten in the nation" and maintaining the tradition at its main booth under the grandstand. She's loved scones, made scones, even shipped them priority mail to such places as Florida and Colorado. "They always made it wherever I sent unbroken," she noted. And when her scone gig comes to an end, Elder will give thanks for the memories. Under the grandstand. That's where she'll be.

AUTHOR'S NOTE: *Leona Elder answered one age-old question people have: How come my scones don't come out as good as yours when I make them at home? She's told people the key is in the mixing. "Don't mix the ingredients by hand. Use an electric mixer. That's what we do." The scone booths put the mix and water in a huge bowl-shaped cauldron and use a power mixer for at least eight minutes to get the dough right.*

A.J. MILLIKEN MANAGED HIS SCONE CREWS WELL

A.J. Milliken didn't know what a Fisher scone was when he was asked if he wanted to manage a scone-making crew at the South Building on the Puyallup fairgrounds for the Western Washington Fair. He certainly knows what a Fisher scone is now, marking in 2022 his sixteenth year as a scone manager for the big fair, rebranded several years ago as the Washington State Fair. "I really had no idea what a scone was," Milliken admitted. "I just knew it was food and I'd had lots of experience as a food manager." Longtime scone worker/manager Ken Zugner, who had forged a partnership with Milliken a few years before the request, was glad to get his friend on board. Milliken was excited to talk about his evolution as a food manager. "I had my first job at fifteen managing an ice cream shop inside a Fred Meyer Store in Longview (WA)," he recalled. "My first boss taught me how to do the books and mop floors." Those were two important things, Milliken, noted, and that good management experience set him off in the right direction. But that boss also shared wisdom on how to deal with customers—common folks and important people and shared stories of a big-time friend, Academy Award–winning actor Walter Brennan, with whom he founded a credit card company. All of this gave the teenage Milliken a sense of storytelling that would serve him well come his scone days much later. Milliken went on to manage other food places,

A.J. Milliken, a longtime scone manager, cares about his workers and displays a determined philosophy to satisfy the appetites of Fisher Scones customers. *Photo by author.*

including a Wendy's, a Denny's, a chicken outlet in Arizona and a restaurant called Stuffy's. "I always got management jobs," Milliken said, adding, "I've always been lucky and fallen into jobs."

Despite his vast experience, Milliken acknowledged that he didn't know what to expect at the Puyallup Fair, an incredibly busy fair, something he was soon to find out as a first-time manager there on the night shift. "I couldn't believe the long lines, which indicated to me that Fisher scones had a cult following," said Milliken, working hard with a crew to move product from the oven to the hot table to customers' hands. "After that first year, I realized that I had to work harder to fine-tune stuff in order to get scones out of the oven and to the counter and customers more quickly, to improve customer service." Meanwhile, Ken Zugner continues to do his tasks on the fairground, and by 2022, he had amassed more than three decades on the scone front. Milliken and his crews continued to improve and became an effective force selling scones at the South Building, where Milliken has managed exclusively. That location has a huge oven, as does the site under the grandstand, and can, at full capacity, bake thirty trays each containing forty scones.

Milliken said he has had so many good employees but pointed to the middle years of his sixteen-year tenure as the best period for consistent good work and memories. "It was such a grand time," he recounted. "We had students who were homeschooled, and they were hardworking, great ethics, supported by their families. The best workers in the world. We gave so many of them their first jobs, responsibility. I miss them all." Their signatures are part of a huge artistic banner that is a permanent fixture on a wall of the South Building, along with mine and that of my son Keith. I worked as a baker. Keith was one of the best dough makers Milliken said he ever saw. Milliken was personable, a testament to his lifetime of heading food crews, and he made the work, which could be strenuous at times, as enjoyable as possible. He frequently jumped on the hot table, telling stories and jokes to the workers. He had trivia contests and guessing games for employees to

The author and Robert Wilkins working the South Building oven during a fall fair. *Photo by Keith Erickson.*

ponder during their breaks, with prizes offered to winners. He occasionally pulled out his own money and gave it to workers for use on the "extreme scream" carnival rides. He knew how to treat his workers with dignity and respect. He appreciated them all.

Asked to recall a humorous anecdote, he recounted a time that he and Zugner had to fix the oven under the grandstand. Over years in the food business, Milliken often had to repair machinery, so working on an oven on the fairgrounds was nothing new. "It was noisy and busy and the restaurant building scone place was providing product for the grandstand," Milliken said. "We closed off the area around the oven and went inside the oven." Their task was to replace a broken sprocket, a very messy job that took several hours. Milliken said he and Ken came out of the back room to a busy and noisy group of workers and customers and shouted, "The oven is fixed!" Dead silence. People seemed shocked. When they looked at each other and themselves, Milliken and Zugner realized they were the ultimate grease monkeys with grease on their faces, arms and clothing, head to feet.

Milliken has an opinion about the legacy of scones. "It's a feeling people get," he maintained. "Scones are a tradition. They bring people in. There is a love for scones and that's honorable and historical. It gives people a warm,

Left: Ken Zugner, an invaluable Fisher Scones manager for more than three decades, is the go-to person who can be counted on to do everything necessary to make Conifer successful during the fair. *Photo by author.*

Right: Debbie Crowell and A.J. Milliken work the hot table inside a scone trailer. *Photo by Keith Erickson.*

fuzzy feeling. I believe you'd be hard put to find a product that comes close to scones at any of the fairs around the country. My prediction is that scones will be around so long as the Puyallup Fair is here and there is a memory of a good product that people can get at a fair price." As for his own legacy, Milliken mused, "The legacy I want to leave is that I maintained excellent standards of service, treating customers and employees well, offering a good product and having fun every day."

KATHIE DENTON REMEMBERS GOOD TIMES

For workers making and selling the famous Fisher scones, the experience was often an "all in the family" occurrence, whether joining with blood relatives to create the delicious morsels or developing a feeling of family among coworkers. Such was the case for Kathie Denton, a woman who worked for Conifer Specialties off and on for two decades. Talking to me from her residence in Graham, Washington, in 2022, she recalled that she was in her late forties when she began her scone career "for Ben [likely Ben Loftin, brother-in-law to Ron Wise, one of Conifer's owners] in the South Building." The South Building was built in the 1970s on the south part of the fairgrounds in Puyallup.

Denton's first scone task was making dough, a process that begins by mixing flour and water in a huge cauldron-like mixer and then entails dumping the dough on a table, weighing the dough into individual dough balls ten ounces each (and no more than ten and a half ounces), rolling the dough balls, flattening them and cutting them into four equally sized triangular pieces. Those pieces are then put on metal trays, forty to a tray, and popped into the oven. It was something that came easy to Denton, who had previously worked as a baker for several grocery stores, including Safeway, Albertsons and Mega Foods. The scone crew became like family, all devoted to producing a quality food item. But later, as her scone endeavors progressed, Denton worked for her mother, Ruth Wilcher, manager of the Green Gate trailer on the Puyallup fairgrounds, and Denton's sister, Laurie Wilcher, worked there, too. "I remember that Ken [Zugner, a Conifer veteran of more than three decades] said he had jobs for me and Momma. I have great memories of working with my best friend [Momma]. She was easy to work with, and we just did our jobs." Denton worked for her mother for two years, and then her mother retired. When her mother died in 2007 at the age of eighty-one, Denton said, someone "made a huge scone as big as a cake for those in attendance" at a memorial service. "No one ever 'fessed up to baking it," she said. But what a wonderful legacy to Ruth Wilcher's scone life.

Kathie Denton continued on, working mostly on the Puyallup fairgrounds and adding various locations, including trailers at the Orange Gate and at Sillyville. But eventually, Denton worked events outside Puyallup, such as the King County Fair and the Highland Games, both in Enumclaw, Washington. "I recall working long hours at the King County Fair, from 9:00 a.m. to 9:00 p.m., and the trailer was located in the sun, no shade, and it was extremely hot and tiring." Denton appreciated the kindness of Ken Zugner when her sister, Laurie, was battling ovarian cancer and also diabetes, the latter resulting in the amputation of one leg below the knee. "Ken was so considerate, saying, 'Of course, Laurie can work,' and she did it in a wheelchair," Denton recounted.

She had fond memories of her scone family, particularly Jean Olson when Olson was managing the Sillyville trailer and with Angie Nelson at various

Kristin Clare (*left*) and Kathie Denton loved their experience making and selling scones. *Photo by Keith Erickson.*

locations, including the Fisher Scones food truck. Denton especially enjoyed being the cashier on the food truck, and her personable nature shone through as she interacted with customers. Her best moments? "One of the challenges was teaching first-timers how to make scones, Denton said. "Teaching them how to pop open scones, insert the butter and raspberry jam, then slide the scone to the bagger. I often corrected people who picked up the scones to insert butter and jam. 'No, No! Slide it down the table, it's easier and faster.' They didn't get it. But then, it was like a light bulb went on and they got it. That was a reward for me." Denton can't forget her scone life. "Seeing people do well, becoming friends, that was the joy," she said, smiling and remembering.

SCONES KEPT KRISTIN CLARE CLOSE TO HER SONS

For Kristin Clare, working scones was all about having the opportunity to spend time with her three sons—Ethan, Micah and Gideon—and enjoying the experience with them, together. She started in 2014 at the South Building on the Puyallup fairgrounds and gave it up during the pandemic. In 2022, her husband, a navy veteran, retired from his civilian job as an electrician, and the couple planned to move to Florida. Their sons are out on their own. She has good memories of working scones with her sons. "Being able to work with my kids together and have that special time with them," Clare said, "that meant a lot." Often, her sons' friends were working, and she got the chance to be part of that unique situation, as well. Furthermore, Clare was instrumental in getting visiting Central American students jobs at the South Building on A.J. Milliken's crew. My son Keith and I worked for A.J., too, and we saw firsthand the care and concern Clare had for the young people working scones. They loved her in return. Clare told me they affectionately called her "Mama Clare." Why did that not surprise me? She acted in a motherly way.

The workplace environment in any scone location can be very busy, and the South Building during Clare's tenure was certainly that with two bakers running the oven at full capacity (thirty trays each with forty scones), two hot tables running with six people each (three on a side), a dough-making operation with at least four people, two cashiers to handle transactions and multiple runners to complete orders. And two lines of customers fifty

The legacy of scone workers lives on with their signatures on an art piece decorating the inside wall of the Puyallup Fair South Building. *Photo by author.*

feet long. Thus, there was no time to waste. But A.J. reduced the stress with his deft handling of everything, Clare recalled. Frequently, A.J. would jump on the hot table, where Clare was, and help out to get the scones off the table and into the baggies to sell. "A.J. made it fun," she recounted, "and would tell jokes or stories." A.J. was utilizing skills learned from previous restaurant managerial positions. He also held trivia contests with prizes and guessing games of various workers' backgrounds for the crew to attempt to answer during ten minutes of half-hour lunch breaks. "It was fun with A.J.," Clare said. "Such a character. But very good with people."

Kristen Clare said most of her memories "have to do with A.J. and everyone working well together." She reemphasized his kindness that made things run smoothly and his willingness to allow her to work with her sons, a "special" time. Furthermore, she's happy that she will be part of a historic crew legacy, explaining, "My signature is on an artistic sign on the wall with those of my sons and many others" who worked scones at the South Building.

THE OSBORNS RECALL MAKING SCONES
AT MEEKER DAYS

Often throughout the past decades, community organizations would have the opportunity to work in Fisher Scones booths and trailers at various events and festivals to raise funds for their groups, in a generous gesture on the part of those responsible for bringing the famous treats to the Pacific Northwest. Puyallup educators Wayne and Robin Osborn vividly recall their experiences for several years making and selling scones at Meeker Days, a street fair celebrating the founding of the city of Puyallup and its pioneer settler Ezra Meeker. "I helped Robin when her women's singing group, the Jet Cities Chorus, worked the scone wagon, teaming up with a men's a capella group, the Harmony Kings," said Osborn. After working the scone wagon, the Osborns gained a new appreciation for the effort it takes to make the popular scones, as well as the overwhelming love for the delicious delicacy enjoyed by customers for a lifetime. "It's backbreaking work, standing on your feet for hours at a time," said Wayne, noting that he'd done all the jobs: cashier, making the dough, cutting the scones and placing them on trays, running the oven as the baker and the buttering and jamming detail. "I liked cutting scones and placing them on the tray best," Wayne said. "The baker position was the most stressful because you had to really pay attention to what you were doing. You didn't want to screw up the whole operation by undercooking or overcooking the scones."

Rain or shine, customers came. The Osborns noted that even on rainy mornings at Meeker Days, when there weren't many folks around yet, a few people always managed to wander up to the scone wagon and inquire when scones would be available. "They had to have their scones, almost like an addiction," opined Wayne. Robin added, "Most of our memories are of customers happy after they got their scones. It seemed like scones always put smiles on people's faces." She said some members of her singing

Left: Twenty-five pounds of dough is mixed in a huge cauldron-like bowl. *Photo by author*.

Right: Dough is weighed, rolled and flattened. *Photo by author*.

group weren't as enthused because it was hard work in a hot scone wagon, and eventually it just became too difficult to get volunteers, so the scone fundraisers for her singing group came to an end.

The Osborns said they and their crew would throw scones that got broken or were too small into a container for use as the base for strawberry shortcakes, or they'd butter and jam them and eat them at break time. "You'd think that after being around scones all day, you'd be sick of them, but, no, they were just as delicious after a few hours" Wayne said. Customers would claim scones were smaller than they remembered or that the recipe had been changed, but Wayne and Robin disagreed. "I don't think so," Wayne wrote in a text message, adding, "They're certainly more expensive than they used to be, but what isn't? LOL! Scones rule!"

Fond memories of Fisher scones go back to their childhood. Wayne and Robin Osborn remember the "long, long, crazy long lines" associated with waiting for scones at the Puyallup Fair. "I think that very rarely have we ever encountered a scone wagon that didn't have a long line." Why do the Osborns love scones so much and why do they think others do as well? "To us, there's nothing better than a hot scone, fresh out of the oven," Wayne

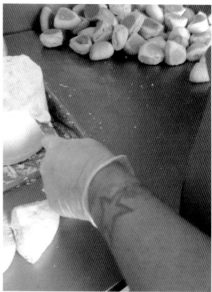

Left: Dough is then cut precisely into four even triangular pieces and placed on trays, which go in the oven. *Photo by author.*

Right: Each baked scone is buttered, jammed and placed in a small glassine bag. *Photo by author.*

declared. "We like them because they're unique; there's nothing quite like them." Then, Wayne got particularly profound in his and his wife's assessment of Fisher scones, proclaiming, "Scones are relatively rare. The stars have to line up just right for you to be able to buy them. Scones are delicious. The combination of hot, baked dough smothered in butter and raspberry jam is just about the greatest thing ever." And that's got to be just about the best endorsement anyone has probably ever given.

Sally Lonn Made Miniature Scone Booth

You've all heard the sayings: "Think big to get big results," "believe big for success," "dream big and your big dream will come true." And so on. Don't tell Sally Lonn, an Arizona woman by way of Washington State, who thinks "small," and that's gotten her big-time notice in the world of miniature art creations and a huge—or should I say, "big"—fan base because of her tiny Fisher Scone booth constructed in 2015 to celebrate the one hundredth anniversary of the scrumptious scones launched to the public by Seattle's Fisher Flouring Mills. The scones were featured at the 1915 Panama-Pacific Exposition in San Francisco and then debuted at the fair in Puyallup. Lonn built the small scone booth for a contest on the national website of Create. miniatures.org. What inspired her to create a scone booth miniature? "I was thinking one day about growing up in the Seattle-Bellevue area and some of my favorite things," Lonn said. "I really loved Fisher scones. So delicious. A real treat. And it still is. Truly a favorite." Her first remembrance of buying and eating a scone was as a teenager in 1962, when she and her cousin were allowed to go the World's Fair in Seattle without parents. "So good" was her tasteful response to that memory. About that same time, she started making miniature figures with paper and wire and really enjoyed the experience. While her youthful passion provided an outlet for her creative juices and produced interesting characters, it eventually went away as she grew into adulthood and became a schoolteacher; married her husband, Howard; and later began raising a family. "Miniatures took a backseat to my life," Lonn recalled. But she couldn't keep them totally away, and they found room in her existence, especially when Lonn began putting together a large dollhouse that "reminded me of one my mother had." That activity spurred Lonn to take classes at a store in Seattle specializing in miniatures, a store long closed. As a result, her interest was definitely rekindled; she joined the National Association of Miniature Enthusiasts (NAME) and has been an active member for many years.

Sally Lonn created a miniature Fisher Scone booth using material she obtained from Conifer Specialties. *Courtesy of Sally and Howard Lonn.*

When Lonn learned that the one hundredth anniversary of Fisher scones was imminent, she became inspired. "I went to the Fisher Scones office (Conifer Specialties) to talk to someone," she recalled. "They were excited and gave me a scone bag and other materials for my purpose. They gave me permission to use the Fisher Scones logo." The booth is small, like a container or cube that holds a baseball, she noted. She made everything, including "the servers and shoppers, and even the tiny bags." Lonn acknowledged that the "rain got to us," and she and her husband moved to Arizona and are currently living in Sun City Grand, a special community within the City of Surprise. But she misses Fisher scones, longing for them when she knows the dates during the summer that the fairs are in operation in Washington State. "I see my brother, a niece and family members when we visit Washington, and I've been known to carry scones back with me to Arizona," she mused. She and her husband, who also grew up in Seattle and remembers the scones as well, have a "big" appetite for a treat they have loved all their lives. Her miniature scone booth is a legacy to those satisfying memories.

SHARING STORIES ABOUT FISHER SCONES

Once a person eats a Fisher scone, he or she is hooked. A sconeaholic. A scone junkie. There have been so many stories from Fisher scone aficionados that support that conclusion. Young kids are introduced to scones by their parents, and they love the hot pastry with butter and raspberry jam. When they grow up and become parents, they give scones to their kids. Usually, those kids become scone lovers, too. And the infatuation is passed on. Scone workers making and selling scones over the years, first for the Fisher Mills Flouring Company and later for Conifer Specialties, have heard so many related stories filled with scone love as sweet as the jam itself inside the tasty biscuit. But there are some stories that stand out because of a life fulfilled by not only consuming scones but also steadfast loyalty and sharing with others. Here are a few:

JOHN WREDE, a longtime Tacoma resident who is a truck manufacturing assembly line inspector, and his wife, Kimberly, a retired hospital emergency room surgical technician who sings in a country band, have enjoyed Fisher scones for five decades. "I went to the Puyallup Fair for the first time in 1973,"

John and Kimberly Wrede visited the 2022 Washington State Fair to get scones to eat and share with friends. *Photo by author.*

Wrede recalled. "I had a scone, I think it was thirty-five cents, and it was great. I haven't missed a fair since then, except when it was shut down for COVID." Sometimes, he and his wife go together to the fair; other times, he goes alone. But when he's by himself, he carries a reminder from his wife to bring back scones for her. He said he and his wife love to get a couple dozen scones and eat some and pass out others to friends. "We appreciate them and think scones are one of the best things the fair has going for itself," Wrede maintained. He noted that his wife would often share scones with the surgical team she was part of and members of the band, 8 Second Ride. The name of the band is drawn from the amount of time a rodeo cowboy must stay on a bucking bronc or a bull to get a score. Asked about amusing stories about scones, Wrede would only say, "Let's just say I have some friends who track me down and give me scones, but I'm not revealing any names."

DOUG AND LOIS QUAYLE, a University Place couple, have loved Fisher scones for many years and either get some at the fair in Puyallup or have friends occasionally bring them scones. Doug, who volunteers to do trail maintenance in the Olympic National forest, and Lois, a retired schoolteacher, like to be in the outdoors hiking. Well, one day a number of years ago, they were hiking on the Pacific Crest Trail near 5,400-foot Chinook Pass on a fall day. As part of their lunch, they had four Fisher scones they had purchased at the fair. They ran across two hikers determined to finish their Pacific Crest Trail hike, which started at the California-Mexico border, and heading for the Washington-Canada border. The Quayles offered each a scone. A surprise treat. One hiker was familiar with Fisher scones, being from Yakima (WA). The other, from out of state, wasn't. They both enjoyed the scones and thanked the Quayles for sharing.

During the 2022 fair, Conifer Specialties held a contest, asking people to post scone stories on its Facebook page and offering free scones to the winners. Here are the winners and their stories:

JADE KNAPP of Puyallup: "I was very pregnant with my son. I was having contractions, but I told my other kids if I go into labor, we need to stop by the booth and get scones first. LOL. I thought I might go into labor in line. Luckily, the baby stayed put, and I got scones. Dedication."

CANDICE CROSETTO of Eatonville: "My father transferred to McChord Air Force Base in the fall of 1965. He got fair tickets, a wonderful surprise. We went as a family and had our first scones. They've been a staple ever since, and I've hit up the scone wagon a few times. The last time I did, I took almost a full baker's dozen (I had to keep a few for me) to an adult home where my mother was living. Many of the ladies who worked there had never had one."

ELDRIDGE RECASNER of Bellevue: "I stood in line at the Puyallup [Washington State] Fair in the rain, and when I finally got to the front of the line, the power went out. But I got the last baker's dozen of scones on September 17, 2021."

The South Building on the Puyallup fairgrounds was aglow on a fall night for concertgoers to stop and purchase scones before or after the grandstand show. *Photo by Keith Erickson.*

LINDA SHOOK of University Place: "From February 6 through May 5, 2016, I was in the hospital and rehab facility after back surgery. The highlight was my family and friends bringing me Fisher scones from the Spring Fair. There were so many that staff put them in freezers at the facilities so I could have scones as needed. It was so wonderful."

Those are a few testimonials about Fisher scones. Just ask people and you'll get a hundred more.

PART VII

SURVIVING:
TWENTY-FIRST-CENTURY SCONE THOUGHTS

Long Lines and Long Memories, Some Amusing

It's only a triangular-shaped biscuit. That's all. This was the first thought of my son Keith and me as we began our scone-making career in 2006 at the big fair in Puyallup, Washington. Keith was learning how to correctly make the dough: adding the right amount of water so it wouldn't be sticky or dry, but somewhere in between. Once the flour and water were in a huge cauldron-like metal bowl, turn on the power mixer for about eight minutes. Then, dump the big pile of dough on the dough table and weigh out ten-ounce clumps. Next, roll the dough into smooth balls without cracks and divots, flatten them and cut them precisely in order to create four evenly shaped triangles. But it's only pieces of dough at that point. After placing forty of them on a metal tray, put them in the oven. That was my job, the baker: watching the oven. Sometimes, the oven doors of the various trailers and fairgrounds' locations had windows that made it easy to watch the scones baking. Others had solid doors, and you had to guess when to check on the scones, knowing that, on average, the scones are done in roughly thirteen minutes. So, you open the oven and check. If you can pop open the largest one on a tray and you don't see doughy strings, then the tray of scones is done and you dump the tray on the hot table's metal surface. Those workers butter, jam and bag the scones. My son and I change our thoughts. No longer is it only a triangular-shaped biscuit. It is a warm, wonderful pastry ready for someone to scarf down

The often busy South Building night crew. *Photo by Keith Erickson.*

and enjoy. People look forward to a scone as much today as they did more than a century ago.

Keith and I became good at our jobs over the years, but we also learned how to ably perform all of the other tasks—hot table, cashier, runner, putting bagged scones in larger takeout bags, driving the food truck, managing crews. We worked at the fair in Puyallup when it was called the Western Washington Fair and later when it was rebranded as the Washington State Fair. Other fairs we have worked at together include the Evergreen State Fair in Monroe, the King County Fair in Enumclaw and the Pierce County Fair in Graham. Other events held on the fairgrounds in Puyallup included the Washington Sportsmen's Show, A Victorian Country Christmas Festival and the Good Guys Car Show. And there have been so many places with the food truck: the Taste of Tacoma and the Bite of Seattle, two events that showcased the food delicacies of hundreds of vendors. Here is a good story from those two a few years back, before the pandemic. Judges came around asking for a dessert item they could judge. We didn't give them a scone, although scones are wonderful. We gave them our fantastic strawberry shortcakes—a broken scone and a half as the base in a bowl, strawberries on top and loads of whipped cream. Guess what? We won best dessert at both events. See, we get some scones that don't get to be scones because they're too small, too crumbly, whatever. Why toss them? That's a waste of money and product. The scones become part of the shortcakes. Later, we moved away from bowls and started putting the shortcakes in cups since cups had a larger capacity that offered customers more yummy ingredients than in a bowl and the possibility of a lid if they were not eating the shortcakes immediately but taking them home. Once other people in line saw a shortcake being sold and its size, it always triggered a rise in orders of that delicious dessert.

There have been so many anecdotes from countless days spent making and selling scones. Some people don't just relish the taste of scones but are hooked by the very aroma of the delicacy. Like one young woman who grabbed me as I was winding through a huge crowd at the fairgrounds in Puyallup one sunny day of the fall fair. She brought me to a halt, thrust her face into my white work shirt and exclaimed, "I had to smell the scones on your shirt. Oh, thank you." She looked intently at me, her eyes sparkling, a smile across her face as she shook her long red hair. "I just love the smell." I stammered that she could come down to the South Building where I was working as the baker, and she could get in more whiffs. She said she had gotten enough to satisfy her, let go of my shirt with both of her hands, gave me a thankful glance and walked by me. I moved on, not looking back as I returned to work.

Yes, people love Fisher scones, but when they see a strawberry shortcake using broken scones as the base, they also get very excited. Shortcakes have won best dessert at the Taste of Tacoma and the Bite of Seattle. *Photo by Dave Bugg.*

Sometimes, people like to take advantage of a long line to present a problem. At least that was my take on a situation that occurred when an older woman came back with a bag of scones. Earlier, I remembered interacting with her and observed her colorful fashion statement, unmatched clothing of red, purple, yellow and green. "These scones are cold," the woman complained. Of course they are, you've been walking around for hours after buying them, I thought. With a customer line fifty yards long, it was no time to create an argument. I disarmed her by taking her bag containing less than the baker's dozen (thirteen) she had purchased, giving her a replacement bag of thirteen hot scones and saying, "Here you go!" Scones such as those returned cannot be resold, so workers take them home at the end of their shifts. That led to a funny situation for me when our Siamese cat, Maddie, displayed her love of scones by getting halfway into a scone takeout bag to eat some scones, and I took a photo. She eats the biscuits but prefers them with butter only, no jam, just like some of our customers do.

RUMINATIONS OF A JOURNEYMAN SCONE TECHNICIAN

Fisher scones are a taste of nostalgia, a reminder of simpler times. In a world full of crises, pandemics and uncertainty, they bring comfort and a hope for return to familiarity. These scones occupy a place in the psyche. It's a part of the human geography and popular culture of the West Coast, mainly due to availability and tradition.

Many have shared their tales with me over the years as I rang up their orders as cashier for one of the half dozen or so booths on the Puyallup fairgrounds. One customer mentioned being snowbound, unable to leave, but remembered there were scones in the freezer. "Just thaw, warm up, eat." Fisher scones came through in a pinch. Now in my experience, scones never lasted as long frozen as the raconteur's, but each person's mileage may vary.

I mentioned scones being a source of hope. During the early days of the COVID-19 pandemic, Conifer Specialties, the company that runs Fisher Scones, needed workers for the food truck. I returned to drive on selected days, thus there would be three separate crews that would not interact with one another in case something happened. We parked outside grocery stores, essential businesses. One man stopped by upon exiting with necessities. "One scone." He had to have a bit of normalcy in a period of anxiety and fear. One scone became a half dozen.

Masked during the pandemic in 2020, Keith Erickson stands outside the scone truck, a valuable tool that brought Fisher scones to the public when fairs were closed. *Photo by author.*

In any theater production there are stagehands, unsung heroes behind the scene orchestrating events and fixes so that the main act, visible to the audience, goes off without a hitch. Ken Zugner personifies that role for Fisher Scones today. He arrives before anyone else, making sure the ovens are working and go up to temperature. If anything requires troubleshooting, he will do it or knows someone who can. A needed delivery shipment of supplies quickly finds its way to booths on fairgrounds or to a truck location. Ken managed the Blue Gate and remained a fixture selling scones at the Bellevue Arts Fair. Ken once said a perk for his length of service with Conifer Specialties was a guarantee of a good hotel room when on the road, and they paid for his cable.

In 2016, Conifer Specialties brought back the food truck concept. You cannot make it to a fair? We might pay a visit to your area. Check social media. A previous mobile scone wagon in the 1920s drove across Washington State bringing the warm joy of scones while promoting flour from Fisher Mills. With any vehicle on the roadway or in a parking lot, you need a sense of where you are. Clearance or how high? You don't want to knock off the exhaust stack. Width? By far the most important task besides fueling is to close and lock the window awning. Another driver who shall remain nameless forgot (it was not me in case you are wondering) and clipped the side of a bridge with it. This distorted the awning to the point where latching was an effort. One month later, operator Bob Westlund thought he had secured the awning only to have it pop up and be completely sheared off on a quarrelsome Puyallup lamppost placed inexplicably just inches from the curb. To prevent damage to the window for the next six months, a series of jerry-rigged solutions, such as a cardboard cover or a sheet of Styrofoam, grommets and bungee cords, were implemented. Thankfully, the duration of the fall Puyallup Fair gave enough time for much-needed repairs without postponing too many other road events. Bob Westlund said he enjoyed piloting the food truck around the South Sound.

"Keeps me active in my retirement." The money working for Conifer "helps out when the fair doesn't employ lawnmowers during the wet months." The success of the food truck concept led Conifer directors to say, "Let's do it again!" The second modern mobile scone wagon will soon mark its debut. New navigators and crew members are poised to make your day with hot scones, cheaper by the dozen and now even by the half dozen, a savings idea I proposed to management years ago.

A colleague wrote on his résumé when applying for a new full-time job that he wasn't just a laborer or a worker at Conifer Specialties; he was a scone technician optimizing the flow of product to the ideal destination while maximizing efficiency.

Keith Erickson, the author's son, ready for a day of dough making in the scone wagon. *Photo by Pam Erickson.*

His description struck a chord with me. In retrospect, that accurately details my role with Conifer also.

AUTHOR'S NOTE: These are thoughts written by my son Keith Erickson, with whom I have worked many years at Conifer Specialties.

WINNING SCONE CONTEST BOOSTED HER EDUCATION, CAREER

Emily Campen, who lives in Malaga, eight miles from Wenatchee, Washington, on the east side of the Cascade Mountain range, is positive that Fisher Scones played an important part in her achieving her goal of becoming a mental health counselor. That's because in 2011 she won a contest sponsored by Conifer Specialties to guess the day when the 100 millionth scone would be sold at the big fall fair in September in Puyallup. Her prize was three large boxes of Fisher scone mix, but the added bonus was $1,000 that she used to further her education in pursuit of a master's degree in mental health counseling at Central Washington University in

Ellensburg. "I used the money to pay for books but also for gas, as I was commuting [seventy miles] between Wenatchee and Ellensburg," Campen recalled in a conversation with the author in the fall of 2022. "I also baked *lots* of scones for my graduate [program] cohorts that year." She is adamant about the impact of the contest win. "The money and scone mix that I won helped to get me here, and I am forever thankful." The "here" she referred to is her job at a clinic in Wenatchee. "I love my career, and I love being able to serve children and families in my community," she exclaimed.

Growing up in Puyallup, Campen remembered attending the fair every year. "When I was in high school, I worked at the Dairy Barn selling ice cream and had friends who worked at the Fisher Scone booths," she recalled. "We would often bring home leftover scones and put them in the freezer so we could enjoy them year-round." Her familiarity with the fair and love of scones prompted her to respond to the scone guessing contest in 2011. "I had seen the contest online, and I thought why not do it?" Campen said. "But then I almost forgot to enter the contest, finally logged in and picked a day at random. Honestly, I was shocked to hear that I had won. I cannot even remember now what day I picked." Conifer's CEO Mike Maher had

Emily Campen and her daughter, Elliott, visited the Washington State Fair in 2022. *Courtesy of Emily Campen.*

the answer, checking the company's records, finding that Campen had successfully picked September 18.

Rekindling pleasant thoughts of her past experiences, Campen said, "I took my five-year-old daughter, Elliott, to this year's [2022] Puyallup Fair for the first time. I cannot seem to make the transition by calling it the Washington State Fair. Our first stop inside the gates was at the Fisher Scone booth to get scones. They tasted just like I remembered. We plan to make our visits to the fair and the Fisher Scone booth an annual tradition, as it was always such a memorable place for me."

TOURING THE OLD MILLS

While the Fisher Flouring Mills on Seattle's Harbor Island was dedicated to shipping out its flour and other products, a new venue on site, Harbor Island Studios, has emerged. Over the next few years, they seek to galvanize a film industry that has been in decline. Since the studios opened in April 2021, there have been a number of projects, most notably one led by Amy Poehler, well-known comedian/actress/director/producer, according to Kate Becker, who is creative economy and recovery director for King County, which has owned the mills site for two decades. Becker, who has a degree in film production and has focused on film and music activities in Seattle and elsewhere for years while building sustainable communities, was gracious to lead an interested group through the massive waterfront warehouse transformed into a 117,000-square-foot sound stage. Besides myself, the group included Mike Blair, a college professor of film and a filmmaker himself; Frank Blazkiewicz, a video games entrepreneur with an MBA from Cal Poly; Keith Erickson, a historian and photographer; and A.J. Milliken, historian and antique dealer, in addition to his duties as a Fisher Scone manager. In the midst of the tour, Becker was joined by her assistant, Andrea Greenstein, economic recovery project manager for King County.

The spaciousness and incredibly high ceilings of the building stood out as obvious advantages to draw movie, television and music producers to this building. The silence was quite overpowering as well, a feature enhanced by King County workers and contractors who rewired the facility and built interior soundproof walls at a cost of $1.5 million, following King County executive Dow Constantine's 2019 announcement of a "creative economy

Kate Becker leads a tour of the Harbor Island Studios, explaining how the sound stage will attract movie production companies. *Photo by Keith Erickson.*

Mike Blair, a professor of film and a filmmaker himself, chats with group members touring the studios created on the former Fisher Flouring Mills site. *Photo by Keith Erickson.*

The spaciousness of the old mills warehouse is perfect for a sound stage. *Photo by Keith Erickson.*

The Fisher Flouring Mills may be history, but a sound stage brings new life to the site. *Photo by Keith Erickson.*

initiative" to better compete against Portland, Vancouver (BC) and other regional cities for film projects. Becker said additional work is planned on the ceilings to make the former mill space more soundproof, mitigating a sometimes noisy problem due to pesky seagulls on the building's roof. She took the group onto the roof, but there were no seagulls to see, only a beautiful view of the harbor. It made me think of the beauty of Seattle and Puget Sound and other parts of the state where movies and television series have been made on location. But often, the production companies went back to Los Angeles or elsewhere to do work that required better controlling the environment. You can't always count on Mother Nature for perfect weather. Or outdoor sounds can force directors frequently to yell, "Cut!" The last major episodic production in Washington was the TV series *Northern Exposure*, filmed on location in Roslyn but also utilizing a warehouse in Redmond for critical set scenes. The show ran for six seasons, 1990–95.

The Harbor Island Studios sound stage gives production companies the option of starting and finishing projects in one geographic area—on location and inside the sound stage. Especially important is the prospect of local artists having access to the facility, opportunities they couldn't have imagined before. The advantages of a sound stage include control of sound, lighting and environment as well as easier logistics and green screen flexibility. Regarding the latter, the premise behind green screens is fairly straightforward. First, filmmakers shoot against a solid-color background, typically green but sometimes blue. Then in postproduction, visual effects artists tweak that color until it becomes transparent. At this point, background footage and other add-on material can be edited in. The facility is providing a valuable niche for Washington State projects at a time when Hollywood's film industry remains the leader in the world, with continual growth from those in Asia, the United Kingdom, Germany and France as well as fast-paced acceleration by those in some African nations, particularly Nigeria. The Fisher Mills brought in grain from eastern Washington and Montana and turned out flour for America and the world. Harbor Island Studios has the potential to bring in producers to create worthwhile entertainment projects to release to America and the world.

PART VIII

BAKING:
FISHER COMFORT RECIPES

Fisher Recipes for Household Tastes

The cookbooks that the first Mary Mills revised and tested for the Fisher Flouring Mills are still good today despite the fact that you cannot get the most prominent ingredient: namely, Fisher's Blend flour. That flour was the mainstay for so many homemakers' food creations and the key ingredient for the famous Fisher scones for many decades. Published in 1933, the *Fisher's Blend Cookbook* had recipes for breads, cakes, cookies, pastries, pies and puddings. It helped promote Fisher's Blend flour. I wondered how the recipes and baking tips would hold up to the test of time. I made one of the recipes and had a neighbor make two, and they turned out well.

I chose a waffle recipe and was pleased how fluffy and light the waffles came out of my waffle iron. Here's a little secret I discovered for how to keep waffles from getting soft and almost mushy and, instead, retain their dry, crunchy texture. When I put the waffles in the oven at 170 degrees to stay warm, I place a wire pie cooling rack inside a metal pan and lay the waffles on top, creating a space underneath them so the waffles don't touch the bottom of the pan. Here's the Fisher recipe:

Cream Waffles

2½ cups Fisher's Blend flour*, divided
1 tablespoon sugar
1 teaspoon salt
3 egg yolks
4 tablespoons melted butter
1 cup milk
1 cup whipping cream
4 teaspoons baking powder
3 egg whites

Sift and measure 2 cups of the flour. Resift with sugar and salt. Beat egg yolks until thick. Add butter, milk, whipping cream. Add to sifted flour and beat until smooth. Add baking powder and ½ cup flour to mixture. Adding baking powder at the last enhances the leavening process, and combining it with some flour creates an even distribution to minimize mixing, avoiding clumping if the baking powder is added by itself. Let stand 15 to 20 minutes until full of bubbles. Beat egg whites until stiff and fold into batter. Do not stir again.

Bake in hot waffle iron 2½ to 3 minutes. Depending on size of iron, the yield could be 6 to 10 waffles.

*Fisher's Blend flour is no longer being packed. Conifer Specialties advises that King Arthur unbleached all-purpose flour is closest to the Fisher's Blend flour combination of wheat grains.

My neighbors Ted and Mary Coyle are excellent bakers. In the case of these two recipes from the *Fisher's Cooky Book*, Mary chose the brownies and peanut butter cookies. How can you go wrong with peanut butter cookies? The truth is you can't. They were tasty and crunchy—just right. She deviated from the original recipe, which instructed to make each dough ball the size of a large marble. Too small, Mary thought, and I had to agree. Thus, we changed the "yield" note to be dependent on the size of the dough balls. As for the brownies, they were unlike any brownies I have ever eaten. And that's a good thing. Many times, brownies can be too chewy. Not these. They were crunchy, almost crumbly, but just the way they should be to melt in your mouth. Truly a chocolate marvel.

Brownies
Yield: 1 dozen

¾ cup Fisher's Blend flour*
⅛ teaspoon salt
1 cup walnuts
2 squares chocolate
½ cup butter
2 eggs
1 cup sugar
1 teaspoon vanilla

Unbelievable, melt-in-your-mouth brownies were made by Mary Coyle using a recipe from a 1930s Fisher cookbook. *Photo by author.*

Sift and measure the flour. Resift with the salt. Chop the walnuts fine and add to flour. Melt chocolate and butter over hot water. Beat eggs thoroughly. Add sugar and vanilla. Add chocolate mixture and fold into the flour.

Pour into a well-greased 9-by-9-inch pan and bake 35 minutes at 350 degrees.

*Fisher's Blend flour is no longer packaged. Substitute a high-quality unbleached all-purpose flour. Conifer recommends the King Arthur brand, which is closest to Fisher's Blend flour mixture of wheat grains.

Peanut Butter Cookies
Yield: Depends on size of dough balls

2 cups Fisher's Blend flour*
1 ½ teaspoons baking soda
⅓ teaspoon salt
½ cup shortening

¾ cup peanut butter
I cup brown sugar
I cup white sugar
2 eggs
I teaspoon vanilla extract

Sift and measure flour. Resift with the baking soda and salt. Cream the shortening, peanut butter and sugars thoroughly. Add eggs and vanilla extract, beating thoroughly

Add the dry ingredients. Roll into balls and press down with a fork. The tines of the fork leave ridges on the cookies. Bake 12 to 15 minutes at 375 degrees.

Scrumptious peanut butter cookies were baked by Mary Coyle using a *Fisher Cooky* recipe. *Photo by author.*

*Fisher's Blend flour is no longer packaged. Substitute a high-quality unbleached all-purpose flour. Conifer recommends the King Arthur brand, which is closest to Fisher's Blend flour mixture of wheat grains.

Sometimes, famous people touted their recipes advocating the use of Fisher's Blend flour. Perhaps the most vocal promoter was TV star Betty White, who frequently ventured to Fisher's KOMO Radio-TV stations, mostly in the 1950s and 1960s to create advertising messages. She was depicted on recipe cards used for marketing efforts and exclaimed, "I like Fisher's Blend flour… It's fresh." Here are a couple of recipes she pitched to the public:

Easy-Slice Banana Loaf
Makes I loaf

Set oven to 350 degrees
Besides 2 cups sifted Fisher's Blend flour, you'll need:

I ½ teaspoons baking powder
½ teaspoon baking soda
I teaspoon salt

½ cup sugar
I cup mashed, ripe bananas (two large)
I egg
¼ cup milk
¼ cup melted shortening or salad oil
½ cup chopped walnuts
I teaspoon vanilla

Stir together sifted flour, baking powder, baking soda, salt and sugar in mixing bowl. Make a hollow in the center; add mashed bananas, eggs, milk, shortening or salad oil, walnuts and vanilla. Stir only until all dry ingredients are moistened. Spread into greased and floured 5x9x3-inch loaf pan. Bake 50 minutes or until done. Remove loaf from pan and let cool on cake rack. Wrap in waxed paper before storing.

TV star Betty White promoted Fisher's Blend flour through her recipe cards, including banana loaf. *The Erickson collection.*

Easy-Slice Orange Loaf
Makes 1 loaf

Set oven to 350 degrees
Besides 2 cups sifted Fisher's Blend flour, you'll need:

1 ½ teaspoons baking powder
¼ teaspoon baking soda
1 teaspoon salt
½ cup sugar
½ teaspoon nutmeg
1 egg
¾ cup orange juice
1 tablespoon grated orange rind
¼ cup melted shortening or salad oil
½ cup chopped pecans (optional)

Stir together sifted flour, baking powder, baking soda, salt, sugar and nutmeg. Make a hollow in the center; add eggs, orange juice and rind, shortening or salad oil and pecans. Stir only until all ingredients are

TV star Betty White promoted Fisher's Blend flour through her recipe cards, like this one for orange loaf. *The Erickson collection.*

moistened. Spread into greased and floured 5x9x3-inch loaf pan. Bake 50 minutes or until done. Remove from pan; let cool on cake rack. Wrap in wax paper before storing.

And today, Conifer markets its products to the world.

On the back of the glassine bags that hold Fisher scones, Conifer highlights new products, such as the scone ice cream that's in area stores, as well as new baking mixes, particularly the following listed in late 2022: Cranberry Orange Scone Mix, Maple Cinnamon Scone Mix, Northwest Apple Cake Mix, Harvest Pumpkin Cake Mix and Classic Crepe Mix. Conifer also encourages people to visit its website at www.fisherscones.com for "great tasting" recipes. The city of Sequim on the Olympic Peninsula is home to the annual Lavender Festival. It's interesting that one recent recipe would incorporate lavender as an ingredient. Here it is:

Lavender Lemon Scones
Makes 1 dozen

⅓ cup white chocolate chips
2¼ teaspoons culinary lavender
Zest of 1 lemon
1 18-oz package Fisher Fair Scone & Short Cake Mix
¾ cup plus 1 tablespoon water
½ tablespoon lemon extract
Raw sugar

Mix white chocolate chips, lavender and lemon zest with scone mix. Add water and lemon extract. Stir with wooden spoon. Turn out on well-floured board. Knead five or six times. Divide into three even pieces. Shape each into a 5-inch circle. Cut each into four wedges. Put on baking sheet. Brush with water and sprinkle raw sugar on top. Bake at 400 degrees for 10 to 14 minutes or until golden brown. Cool on wire rack.

FINAL THOUGHTS

The founders of Fisher scones served the pastry treat as an afterthought. It promoted the brands of flour available to purchase, similar to the company's mail order recipe books or a guarantee (You'll like it or your money back!) when making orange loaf. The ownership of Fisher Scones has changed hands. The flour is similar but not exactly like the Blend line Fisher Mills crafted. The Harbor Island mills are defunct, the site slated for redevelopment. Continental-Krusteaz mills in Illinois and Kentucky supply the flour now for their Conifer Specialties business. The Krusteaz line includes Albers Corn Meal, Zoom cereal and Snoqualmie Falls and CB Old Country Store pancake mix. The Fisher TV and radio shows sponsored by Zoom over the airwaves gave way for social media posts about upcoming events at which one can purchase scones. The wooden handle of my grandfather's axe has been replaced and so has the blade. Planks, sails, mast and rivets on the ship of Theseus, too. Piece by piece. Human beings are replenished entirely every seven years or so, cell by cell. Yet our minds seem continuous. We seem to have an everlasting awareness. Fisher scones exist as a continuous role not fulfilled by the original physical entity, Fisher Flour Mills.

Who could have foreseen when O.W. and O.D. Fisher assembled a flour empire more than a century ago that Fisher scones would outlive that legacy? It seems that Fisher scones will go on so long as people remember, and as of this century, they do. They look for the scone wagon locations, at a shopping center or pumpkin patch farm, and also events at fairgrounds

NOVEMBER 29, 1955

TIME
THE WEEKLY NEWSMAGAZINE

MAN OF THE YEAR
OLIVER DAVID (O.D.) FISHER
Milling · Banking · Lumbering · Insurance · Radio · Television

Above: O.D. Fisher, leader of the Fisher family empire after his father's death, is celebrated by everyone close to him as "Man of the Year" on a mock *TIME* magazine cover. *Courtesy A.J. Milliken collection.*

Opposite: In a 2010 photo, Ashley Stamper strikes a Statue of Liberty pose, emphasizing the iconic presence of Fisher scones in the Northwest. *Photo by Keith Erickson.*

because to them, scones represent good in our world. "We saw the scone truck and had to get scones." Despite all the changes over the years, scones remain more than just biscuits. They're a food essential, maybe even worthy of being served on a pedestal, praises sung to the melody of a Bob Dylan tune.

People go out of their way, even change course in their lives, to find Fisher scones. They spot the scone truck while driving out and about on errands, and they turn around, take a diversion, make a beeline for the truck. The smiles on people's faces tell the scone workers the truth behind their motivation. It reflects a genuine love for something that embraces a way of life and tradition. The role of Fisher scones lives on. These scones help people survive uncertain times and calamities, providing hope and keeping fond memories alive. Scones are a part of celebratory events and accomplishments, fulfilling a role. And that's enough.

BIBLIOGRAPHY

Bellingham (WA) Herald. "Fisher Mills Finest Flouring Mills." April 10, 1934.

Dumond, Val. *Doin' the Puyallup: An Illustrated History.* Puyallup: Western Washington Fair Association, 1991.

Eugene (OR) Guard. "Delicious Flaky Biscuits in a Jiffy." July 2, 1936.

Fisher Scones Facebook. "Scone Stories Contest Winners." September 2022.

Honolulu Advertiser. "Fisher Flour Mills Will Serve Scones." October 20, 1924.

———. "Fisher Flour People Here for the Fair." August 14, 1925.

———. "Right This Way—Piping Hot Scones." August 31, 1925.

Honolulu Star Bulletin. "Fisher Flouring Mills Exhibit." September 27, 1924.

———. "Fisher's Blend Good for Cakes and Pastry." October 18, 1924.

———. "Flour Mills Has Three Displays." September 2, 1925.

———. "H.W. Bryan Aid Fairs." October 8, 1924.

———. "Much Interest in Big Contest." November 25, 1924.

Interviews:

    Suzanne Hall. January 26, 2022.

    Sally Lonn. March 2022.

    Wayne and Robin Osborn. April 2022.

    Phelps Fisher. May 18, 2022.

    Mike Maher. June 6, 2022.

    Kathie Denton. June 2022.

    Kristin Clare. August 2022.

    Leona Elder. August 2022.

    A.J. Milliken. September 2022.

Emily Campen. October 19, 2022.

Frances and Dwayne Ryland, October 26, 2022.

Maui Magazine. "All's Fair." September 1, 2013.

Museum of History and Industry (MOHAI). Seattle: Kenneth R. Fisher Interviews, 1985.

Nisqually Valley News. "The Evolution of the Washington State Fair." January 20, 2022.

Northwest Room, Tacoma Public Library. Images of Mary Mills in newspaper advertisement in 1930s, flour being loaded on ship, Fisher's Tacoma warehouse, and Fisher Blend float in parade.

Oregon Daily Journal. "Fisher's Blend Scones." March 6, 1916.

———. "Fisher's Scones." December 16, 1919.

Peninsula Daily News. "Scones Taste Like Fair Time in Clallam County." August 20, 2022.

Pioneergirl.com/archives. "Laura Ingalls Wilder at Panama Pacific Expo." October 14, 1915.

Polk City Directories. Tacoma, Portland, and San Francisco. Northwest Room, Tacoma Public Library.

Seattle Daily Times. "Cake Baking Demonstration Slated Friday." August 9, 1933.

———. "Fisher Mills Now Largest in West." September 16, 1917.

———. "O.W. Fisher Dies at Age of 79." June 23, 1922.

———. "Traveling Oven Brings Scones, Blend Serves 'Em Hot." July 27, 1919.

Seattle Post-Intelligencer. "From Small Foods to Big Plans." October 31, 2005.

Seattle Star. "Fisher Blend Hockey." October and November, 1938.

———. "Fisher's Blend Flour Better Than the Best." May 15, 1912.

———. "Newton Coleman, Widely Known, Dies." October 13, 1922.

Seattle Times. "Do You Know the Sconeman? He's Mike Maher." September 14, 2006.

———. "Fisher Scones Still the Sweetheart of Fair." September 6, 2011.

Spokane (WA) Chronicle. "Special Offer for Scone Cutter." April 14, 1955.

Steen, Herman. *The O.W. Fisher Heritage*. Seattle: Dogwood Press Production, 1961.

Stone, Mike. *Pixies in the Valley: Oregon's Pixie Kitchen and Pixieland*. West Conshohocken, PA: Infinity Publishing, 2010.

Tacoma Daily Ledger. "Cooking Class Near Capacity." October 17, 1935.

———. "Headquarters Is Now in Tacoma." December 15, 1918.

———. "Motor Car Helps Create Market." September 28, 1919.

———. "Something to Eat for Everyone." September 12, 1920.

Tacoma News Tribune. "Great Fair Opens to Crowds." September 16, 1946.
———. "Scone Mix on Market." September 18, 1954.
———. "There No Longer a Nickel, but Still So Yummmm." September 9, 2011.
Tiffany Transcription. "Zoom Cereal Sponsored 1946 Radio Show." Middle Tennessee State University collection.
Tulare (CA) Advance-Register. "You Can Have These Famous Fisher's Blend Scones at Home." March 24, 1916.
Waterfront Workers History Project. University of Washington collection.
Zander, Julie McDonald. *Chapters of Life at the Southwest Washington Fair.* Chehalis, WA: Chapters of Life, 2015.

ABOUT THE AUTHOR

Jim Erickson has been a writer all his life, mostly for newspapers, particularly the *Tacoma News Tribune*, and with two Washington State government agencies. He has won writing and photography awards. Most prestigious was a national award for the best energy publication in the United States, in competition with other states. He has a bachelor's degree in journalism and a master's degree in education. As a teacher, he emphasized writing in all subjects. After nearly two decades working for Conifer Specialties, mostly as a baker, his coworkers have dubbed him the "Scone Wizard." He lives in Tacoma, Washington.

Visit us at
www.historypress.com